Conscription 1917

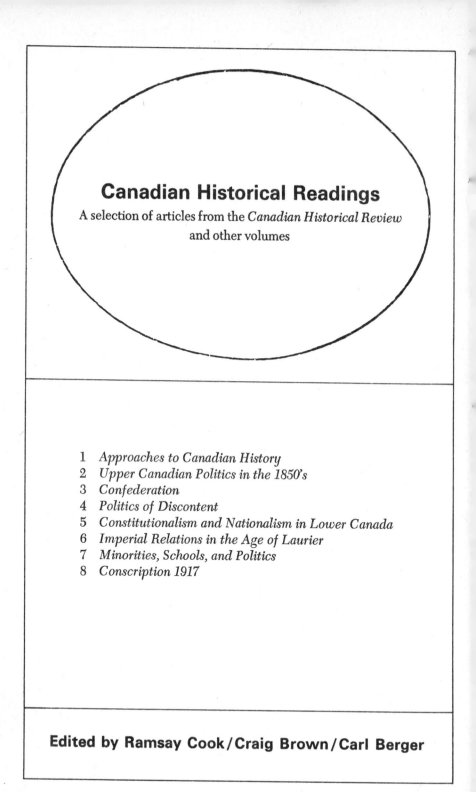

Canadian Historical Readings

A selection of articles from the *Canadian Historical Review*
and other volumes

Edited by Ramsay Cook / Craig Brown / Carl Berger

Conscription 1917

Essays by A. M. Willms / Ramsay Cook
J. M. Bliss / Martin Robin

Introduction by Carl Berger

University of Toronto Press

© University of Toronto Press
Printed in Canada
SBN 8020 1618 9

Contents

Introduction

CARL BERGER

FEW EVENTS REVEALED the fragility of Canadian unity so dramatically as the conscription crisis of 1917. Canada entered the Great War enthusiastically and innocently: no one questioned the rightness of a struggle to preserve France and the Empire and to exterminate German militarism. In a legal and constitutional sense Canada was at war because Britain was at war, but psychologically and emotionally Canadians were at war for varied reasons. Over two-thirds of the volunteers in the first contingent were British-born who enlisted to fight for the homeland. Some Canadians welcomed participation as an opportunity for national self-assertion; others saw the conflict as a Canadian war to preserve those same values that the allies defended. French Canadians were told that it was their duty to discharge the historic obligations to France and Britain, especially to Britain, which had guaranteed their liberties, language, and faith.

As the war of attrition dragged on and the demands upon manpower grew beyond all forecasts, even the illusion of unanimity was shattered. Popular support in French Canada diminished because of mistakes in war organization, the early failure to form French-Canadian regiments, and the recrudescence of the Ontario schools issue which convinced French Canadians that their real enemies were across the Ottawa River, not the Atlantic ocean. For over a decade Henri Bourassa and the *nationalistes* had saturated Quebec with an indictment of imperialism. Early in 1915 the attack was resumed and Bourassa wondered whether French Canadians had any reasons for being grateful for the repeated efforts to denationalize them, asserted that the war was at bottom a clash of imperial rivals, and questioned whether Canada should continue to make sacrifices for a cause so unconnected with its true national interest. The presence of the Canadian prime minister on the Imperial Defence Committee appeared as another sly stratagem to centralize the Empire; the announcement in the spring of 1917 that only conscription could maintain the Canadian forces at fighting strength seemed a logical culmination of the whole imperialist campaign. The passage of the Military Service Act, the formation of the Unionist coalition, and the election of 1917 drove a deep wedge between the Canadian peoples and left a legacy of suspicion and bitterness. To French Canadians 1917 was the climax of a long history of defeat; once again a brutal and insensitive majority had violated the tolerant principles of Confederation and imposed its will upon a helpless minority.

The conscription crisis has been subjected to considerable analysis. As in so many other areas of Canadian history, O. D. Skelton's biography of Sir Wilfrid Laurier was of seminal importance for establishing a line of interpretation which was closely followed by many other historians. Skelton sought to sum up the meaning of Canadian liberalism and for him the tragedy of conscription was that it shattered the national unity which had been painstakingly built up in the Laurier period. His was essentially a consensus version of the Canadian past: he tended to minimize the extent of internal divisions and underlined the inevitability of conciliation and compromise. Those who challenged Laurier's search for the middle way, whether they were the Bourassa nationalists or the English-Canadian imperialists, were condemned for their imperfect appreciation of the Canadian reality. For Skelton, one of the chief divisive forces in Canadian life was the sentimental attachment to Britain. It was this sympathy for Britain, he believed, which impelled English Canadians to support the war. Fundamentally, it was not Canada's war at all: the most intensely Canadian people whose ancestral roots ran back the deepest were precisely those who were most opposed to unlimited sacrifices. The advocates of compulsory military service, who engineered Union Government and disfranchised "enemy aliens" and enfranchised the close female relatives of soldiers at the front, were obviously driven by political motives. The purpose of conscription, Skelton wrote, was "not to win the war but to win the election." Conscription, moreover, was needless. It neither provided the additional men nor affected materially the outcome of the war. It unnecessarily split the country and broke up the political instrument in which French and English Canadians had worked together. One lesson which Skelton drew from this experience was that if the national unity of the country was to be preserved Canada must never again become embroiled and entangled in old world conflicts.

The point at issue between Skelton's general argument and more recent approaches concerns the motives of those who supported conscription. In contrast to previous studies, such as Elizabeth Armstrong's *The Crisis of Quebec, 1914–1918* (New York, 1937) and Mason Wade's *The French Canadians, 1760–1945* (Toronto, 1955) which concentrated upon the opposition in French Canada, the articles reprinted here deal mainly with the reaction, both favourable and critical, of English Canadians. And what emerges out of these accounts is not so much a comprehensive reinterpretation of the crisis but rather a series of suggestive insights which extend our understanding, though not necessarily our sympathy. On one level A. M. Willms rejected completely the argument that conscription was unscrupulously exploited by a discredited party to maintain itself in power. Basing his reassessment on the recently available papers of those politicians who supported it as a military necessity, he suggested that they in fact underestimated its appeal and that other and more persuasive considerations entered into their thinking. It will be left to the reader to decide how effectively he has dealt with the charge that the pro-conscriptionists had gone so far in identifying themselves with the national purpose that they were ready to employ virtually any means to maintain their power. All too frequently the conscription crisis is analyzed in terms of political decisions taken at the top with only vague and casual references to the drift of popular opinion in English Canada. In his article on the Methodist Church and the war, and particularly the position of the *Christian Guardian*, J. M. Bliss has examined one important example of popular pressure for conscription and has shown how religious idealism was mobilized in its support. His study also illustrates the complicated connection between the war, conscription, and the reform impulse. It is well-known that farmer and labour discontent was aggravated by conscription, not only because of the cancellation of exemptions after the election, but also, as Martin Robin reminds us, because of the unsatisfied demand that wealth as well as men be conscripted. But what the position of the Methodists illustrates is that the zest for reforming the social order grew out of the same ideological complex as did conscription itself. Finally, the articles by Willms and Ramsay Cook directly challenge the view that those who were most vociferous in demanding conscription simply wanted to "help England." This judgment does not explain why certain Canadian nationalists, like John Dafoe of Winnipeg, believed that Canada was in the war as a nation and major participant, not as a subsidiary and subordinate helper, and that it had to accept the responsibilities contingent upon that status. And this takes us to the core of the problem of the conscription crisis: it represented a clash between different conceptions of Canada. Tragedies of the magnitude of 1917 are not produced by confrontations between good and evil: that it is no longer treated that way is indicative of the growing sophistication of Canadian historical scholarship.

Apart from the surveys by Wade and Armstrong, the most accessible accounts of the conscription crisis are to be found in biographies and memoirs – O. D. Skelton's *Life and Letters of Sir Wilfrid Laurier* (Carleton Library, Toronto, 1965), volume 2; John Dafoe, *Laurier, A Study in Canadian Politics* (Carleton Library, Toronto, 1963) and John Dafoe, *Sir Clifford Sifton in Relation to His Times* (Toronto, 1931); G. R. Cook, *The Politics of John W. Dafoe and the Free Press* (Toronto, 1963); R. Rumilly, *Henri Bourassa, la vie publique d'un grand canadien* (Montréal, 1953); C. Murrow, *Henri Bourassa and French-Canadian Nationalism: Opposition to Empire* (Montreal, 1968); R. MacGregor Dawson, *William Lyon Mackenzie King: A Political Biography, 1874–1923* (Toronto, 1958); W. R. Graham, *Arthur Meighen: The Door of Opportunity* (Toronto, 1960); and H. Borden, ed., *Sir Robert Laird Borden: His Memoirs* (Toronto, 1938), volume 2. The *Canadian Annual Review of Public Affairs* for 1917 edited by J. C. Hopkins (Toronto, 1918) contains a densely detailed contemporary chronicle of the crisis.

The genesis and significance of the Ontario school question which influenced French-Canadian opinion on the war so fundamentally is dealt with in F. A. Walker, *Catholic Education and Politics in Ontario* (Toronto, 1964), and in two articles which have been reprinted in volume 7 of this series, M. Prang, "Clerics, Politicians, and the Bilingual Schools Issue in Ontario, 1910–1917," *Canadian Historical Review*, XLI (December, 1960), and M. Barber, "The Ontario Bilingual Schools Issue: Sources of Conflict," *ibid.*, XLVII (September, 1966). A lively account of activities on the battle front is J. Swettenham, *To Seize the Victory: The Canadian Corps in World War I* (Toronto, 1965); a succinct summary of the election of 1917 is given in J. M. Beck, *Pendulum of Power: Canada's Federal Elections* (Toronto, 1968); and the treatment of the ethnic groups is described in J. A. Boudreau, "Western Canada's 'Enemy Aliens' in World War One," *Alberta Historical Review*, XII (winter, 1964). W. L. Morton, *The Progressive Party in Canada* (Toronto, 1950) places the conscription episode in the context of agrarian protest. Conscription cast a long shadow over the Canadian government's handling of the manpower problem in World War II: this aspect may be pursued in J. L. Granatstein, *Conscription in the Second World War, 1939–1945* (Toronto, 1969). A sensitive and imaginative examination of the war crises in French and English separation may be found in Hugh MacLennan's novel, *Two Solitudes* (Toronto, 1945).

Conscription 1917: A Brief for the Defence

A. M. WILLMS

THE reaction of French Canada to conscription has been treated in some detail by Professor Mason Wade[1] and Miss Elizabeth Armstrong[2] but the story of its effect on the Liberal party and on the election of 1917 has not yet been fully told. Recently the papers of several leading men in this political drama have been made available to historians and they inspire further study of these events. The papers of Sir Wilfrid Laurier trace like a fascinating novel the collapse of the strong Liberal party around its tragic, white-plumed hero. They blame the catastrophe on the political machinations of the Government and contend that conscription was neither necessary nor successful, but that it caused a serious rift between Quebec and the rest of Canada. Thus the Laurier Papers tend to confirm the story of conscription as it has been accepted by Canadian historians. But there are other versions of this story in such collections as the Borden Papers, the Rowell Papers, and the Dafoe Papers. In fact the cumulative effect of new materials is to show that not only was conscription militarily necessary—that Canada's contribution to the fighting lagged behind that of her principal allies and sister Dominions until conscription was employed—but also that the success of conscription was not achieved at the cost of a national tragedy.

One fact that constantly obtrudes on the reader of the new collections is the remarkable political success of conscription. This raises the suspicion that the Military Service Bill was introduced by the Government as a political expedient. There is no absolute evidence to prove or disprove this suggestion, but it deserves fuller examination.

Whenever the members of the federal Conservative party assessed their political stock during the winter of 1916 to 1917 they felt very uncomfortable. The extended life of Parliament was running out and the Government was unpopular with the public. The Liberal party on the other hand was, or appeared to be, strong and confident. The Conservatives were in trouble. Of seven provincial elections held between August, 1915, and June, 1917, they lost seven. In three provinces Conservative governments were ousted and in

[1] *The French Canadians 1760–1945* (Toronto, 1955).
[2] *The Crisis of Quebec 1914–1918* (New York, 1937).

Reprinted from *Canadian Historical Review*, XXXVII (4), December, 1956

all the other elections the Conservatives held fewer seats after the
voting than they had before. In Manitoba and British Columbia
the elections were utter routs. In the latter province the Liberals
had started the year 1916 with no seats in the provincial legislature
and finished with 37 out of 47, and in Manitoba the Conservatives
lost 22 seats, giving the Liberals an over-all majority of 32 seats.
While provincial elections do not always reflect the standing of
federal parties, these were unusually heavy portents. Of the New
Brunswick election Dafoe wrote: "The result in New Brunswick
must have been very discouraging to them, as that was in fact a
trial of strength between the Dominion parties";[3] while a leading
federal Liberal admitted modestly: "Our successes in the provincial
arenas are due solely to the mistakes, corruption and incompetence
of our opponents. . . ."[4]

Federal by-elections are another measure of government popu-
larity. The paucity of by-elections in this period constitutes an
admission of Government weakness; for, while the Conservative
party retained its seats in the three ridings that were opened, the
Government dared not issue writs in the other twenty constituencies
which became vacant between March, 1915, and July, 1917.

There were reasons for the Government's unpopularity. Its weakness and ineptness appeared quite obviously in the Ross Rifle
débâcle. Wartime patronage and profiteering was not proven by a
royal commission or in a court of law, but the Liberal members of
Parliament were not alone in believing the repeated accusations
and in blaming the laxity of the Government. The cost of living
was rising very sharply with the wartime economic boom and the
benefits of higher prices did not accrue to all the population. The
parliamentary Opposition felt that Messrs. Mackenzie and Mann
should not be reimbursed for a railway taken over by the Government when at the point of bankruptcy. Sir George Foster feared
this might make electioneering material,[5] while of the Quebec and
Saguenay Railway purchase he wrote: "The Quebec and Saguenay
mess goes through—an unsavory and absolutely indefensible job—
put through by the Prime Minister in pursuance of arrangements
made with Forget and the Bank of Commerce nearly three years
ago."[6]

The extraordinary personality of Sam Hughes constituted both an

---

[3]Public Archives of Canada, Dafoe Papers, Dafoe to Sifton, Feb. 27, 1917.
[4]P.A.C., Laurier Papers, E. M. Macdonald to Laurier, Sept. 28, 1916.
[5]P.A.C., Foster Papers, Diary, Aug. 16, 1917.
[6]*Ibid.*, May 16, 1916.

internal weakness within the Government and an election handicap. This was almost unanimously admitted on both sides, while the adverse report of Judge Galt on Hon. Robert Rogers' connections with government contracts in Manitoba was honey to the Opposition bears. Of these two ministers Foster asserted: "Both have been loads to carry—neither should have been made minister—for both the party has paid and will pay dearly."[7] The increasing failure of recruiting and the dismal flop of two substitute measures, national service and the semi-active militia, served to increase a general lack of confidence. The Prime Minister was accused of weakness, in-action, and vacillation; "a well meaning incompetent"[8] Dafoe dubbed him, while a member of the cabinet repeatedly denounced his policy of "drift—corroding drift."[9]

The Conservative who looked at the political scene would then turn anxiously to the calendar. The life of Parliament would expire on October 7, 1917, and the belligerent Opposition were not likely to grant another extension. With six months left, Dafoe predicted: "Their defeat when they appeal to the people appears inevitable, unless some new factor enters into the contest and gives them a good battle cry."[10]

The miracle happened. Six months later, a new factor gave Borden and his party not only a great battle cry but a large majority in the election. The Liberal Opposition so strong in January was pitifully weak in December, its leader had offered to resign, and a majority of its outstanding members had left the party or refused it their support. Strong provincial or local Liberal organizations had melted away or deserted intact to the enemy. In 1916 the Liberal party in Saskatchewan had a well-oiled party machine. Its engineer, Hon. J. A. Calder, boasted: ". . . our people are but awaiting the fray. The general federal election cannot be brought on too soon to please our people."[11] A year later, almost to the day, a lone Saskatchewan Liberal appealed for help: "So far as organization goes Calder is the whole thing and his going . . . has left us high and dry."[12] "We are in a bad way here."[13]

In New Brunswick "Fighting Frank" Carvell, the most promising of the young Liberals and a recent nominee to succeed Laurier, took

[7]Ibid., Aug. 17, 1917.
[8]Dafoe Papers, Dafoe to G. M. Wrong, Dec. 12, 1916.
[9]Foster Papers, Diary, Oct. 8, 1915.
[10]Dafoe Papers, Dafoe to Laurier, April 26, 1917.
[11]Laurier Papers, Calder to Laurier, Nov. 8, 1916.
[12]Ibid., Knowles to Laurier, Nov. 6, 1917.
[13]Ibid., Nov. 24, 1917.

his political army over to the Government. In Nova Scotia the astute provincial Premier—Prime Minister five years longer than Mackenzie King—had considered an offer to enter the Union cabinet and had promised to back Government candidates in his province. Laurier lamented his lost follower "whose judgment is so clear and whose sagacity was never at fault."[14] Fielding, the old veteran, the crown prince of the Liberal party, was bewailed in biblical language.[15] In Ontario the provincial Liberal leader was one of the first to join the Borden cabinet, and more ill news soon reached Laurier: "Yesterday it was Pardee and today it will be Graham. Graham and Pardee as dear to me as my own brothers."[16] In Alberta and Manitoba the leading Liberals also deserted, and in Alberta the two remaining Liberal leaders, Oliver and Cross, were by this time bitter foes. In British Columbia the Liberal Premier made overtures to the federal Government. The two great Liberal newspapers followed the traitors, setting an example that was emulated by all but three of the Liberal papers west of the Ottawa River.[17]

This great tribulation was brought on the Liberal party by the announcement of the Government's Military Service bill. It pulled the Borden Government out of the mire and set it on its feet. It split both of the old parties and made Union Government possible. It won the election of 1917 for Borden and company. There were, of course, other factors that contributed to the Government's revival. The ditching of Sam Hughes and Bob Rogers, the last-minute adoption of a mild form of income tax, the slight boosting of an inadequate profits tax; the appointment of a vigorous food controller, though with but limited powers, the admission of wheat and flour tariff-free into the United States, and the fixing of wheat prices at over two dollars a bushel, all helped. The nefarious War Times Election Act also increased the votes for the Government and denied votes to the Opposition. But conscription was the big issue; it acted as a solvent on Liberal party bonds while it brought together an amazing array of political talent in the Union Government. It was the dominant issue before the electors at the polls. In all the provinces of Canada this issue was sentimentalized and exaggerated; it was screamed from the hustings and thundered from the pulpits. Those against it were "cowards and traitors" and those for were

[14]Ibid., Laurier to E. M. Macdonald, Nov. 19, 1917.
[15]H. S. Ferns and B. Ostry, The Age of Mackenzie King (London, 1955), 231.
[16]Laurier Papers, Laurier to A. B. Aylesworth, June 22, 1917.
[17]Edmonton Bulletin, Peterboro Times, London Advertiser: Laurier Papers, Laurier to R. R. Cromarty, Nov. 23, 1917.

"autocrats worse than the Kaiser." Unquestionably, then, conscription proved a wonderful political expedient. But was it nothing more?

A crisis existed. Canada was fighting a war. She was fighting not for England and not for France but for Canada. She was not only defending the principles of right, of justice, and of democracy, but she was also defending Canada's right to these principles. Laurier said of the Canadian soldiers: "They have left their avocations to do battle for a cause which they deem, and rightly deem the cause of freedom . . . to save civilization from the unbridled lust of conquest and domination."[18] Whether Canada was expecting an imminent invasion was immaterial, for, as Foster pointed out, "It makes very little difference if we do not win this war whether the Hun today is three thousand miles away from Canada or only half a mile beyond our coasts. In either case if the Hun wins the ultimate result would be the same."[19] Rowell outlined the basic military strategy involved: "Surely the time has come when we can all recognize that Canada is being defended in Flanders and in France just as truly and much more effectively than she could be defended on the banks of the St. Lawrence."[20]

There is no doubt that the war in 1917 was balancing finely, too finely, in the scales of the future. In the spring of 1917 Russia's vast manpower resources were becoming useless while the fighting potential of the United States could not be mustered immediately. Italy was not always holding her own against Austria, and in the French armies there were mutinies. Even in Britain there was defeatism and some despair as the early over-optimism gave way to dark pessimism. The submarine was wreaking havoc in the Atlantic, while the mighty British navy was vainly casting about for adequate counter measures. Bloody fighting had taken place in 1916 with but small advances by either side, and leaders on both sides were coming to realize that victory must entail further great sacrifices and possibly prolonged and increasing hardships.

With this crisis at hand, was Canada doing all in her power to help defeat Germany? There were many Canadians who contended that Canada had sent overseas as many men as her economy could possibly spare. There were those who claimed that Canada had done enough. Canada had indeed contributed a substantial share to the allied effort; but she had done less than others. In the contribution of manpower she lagged far behind Great Britain and

[18]*Canada, House of Commons Debates,* 1917, III, 2392.   [19]*Ibid.,* 2408.
[20]Laurier Papers, Rowell to Laurier, May 29, 1917.

France, and she had done less than the other Dominions. Straight comparisons, especially with the older countries, are not really valid but the ratios are striking. According to Hon. N. W. Rowell, to equal Australia's effort Canada should have had overseas at the end of January, 1917, 500,000 men; to compare with New Zealand her quota was 450,000, and with South Africa, over 400,000. In actual fact there were 284,000 Canadians in England and France. France and Great Britain had respectively four and three times as many men in the forces in proportion to their population. These figures are difficult to verify. By the end of the war the ratios had changed, but this was mostly because of Canada's great effort in 1918 under the pressure of conscription. But never at any time was Canada suffering seriously from lack of manpower. Her booming economy was one indication. Rowell claimed that "Canada has profited the most and suffered the least from this war of any of the nations of the empire."[21] Individuals were making great sacrifices, but the nation was not, either in manpower or in national wealth.[22]

It is impossible to compare accurately the economy of Canada in the First and Second World Wars. Both periods were eras of great expansion, but the contribution in manpower in the Second World War was proportionately greater. With an increase in population of 50 per cent, her commitment in manpower increased over 60 per cent. Even this greater contribution, however, did not seriously impair Canada's vital industries.

Canada had sent 312,000 men overseas by the end of April, 1917, and in France she was maintaining four divisions with supporting units, a total of more than 125,000 men. The Canadian Government had hoped to send a fifth division to France, but the decreasing enlistment at home prohibited this. To keep the four divisions up to strength, an estimated 10,000 men were required every month as reinforcements.[23] The figures of actual reinforcements available are hard to find and can be deduced only approximately, yet it would seem that at the end of April Canada had reinforcements for approximately six months, under normal circumstances. There were, however, some complications with regard to existing reinforcements. Losses were heaviest in the infantry, but the men available were not all infantrymen. The voluntary enlistment of infantry in the first four months of 1917 was so low that normal wastage in Canada left

[21]Quotation and figures from P.A.C., Rowell Papers, Rowell to Laurier, July 11, 1917.
[22]E. L. Bogart, *Direct and Indirect Costs of the Great World War* (London, 1920).
[23]P.A.C., Borden Papers, OC 499, p. 53524.

very few men for overseas. Thus April and May produced a gross total of 3,000 infantry recruits who still had to be trained, with a percentage of wastage resulting. In these same two months Canadian battle casualties in France were 20,045. Approximately 10,000 of these casualties, or about 80 per cent of the wounded, could be expected to return to the trenches eventually, but the loss of men still exceeded the gain by over 7,000. Normal infantry reinforcement requirements were 7,800 per month.[24] At the rate of the 1917 spring enlistment it would take more than four months' enlistment to make up one normal month's loss—and enlistment had not yet reached its lowest point. These were the figures as they appeared at the time conscription was introduced. In actual fact the existing reinforcements together with the reduced voluntary enlistments were adequate for a year; a year that had, however, much lighter casualties than were expected.

In the meantime the High Command was presenting to the Imperial War Cabinet its urgent requirement for more troops. Borden, Perley, and Kemp, the ministers most closely connected with Canadian military decisions, saw what a strenuous effort the other allies were putting forth; they saw the great need for men at the front but they could not, under the circumstances, commit Canada to the sending of a fifth division. Instead they set themselves the goal of enlisting another 100,000 men. Whether these men could be used to fill out the fifth division or whether they would have to be used entirely in reinforcing the four divisions would depend on military factors and on the speed of enlistment. The need was great and the men were available. How could they be best mobilized?

It would appear that by the spring of 1917 the Canadian Government had exhausted the potentialities of voluntary recruiting. In the first three years of war the Government and the Militia Department had made many mistakes, some of them gross errors in tact and common sense. The greatest offender was the Minister of Militia, but the rest of the cabinet and especially the Prime Minister must share the blame. They had antagonized over-sensitive Quebec; they had authorized the recruiting of units and then broken them up; they had commissioned too many officers and lacked the courage to put them to work or discharge them; they had failed to recruit wealth as they recruited manpower and they had not stopped profiteering or patronage. By 1917 many of these mistakes had become

[24]Figures are from *House of Commons Debates*, 1917, II, 1816; III, 2892; also Borden Papers, OC 332, pp. 39112, 39121, 39128, OC 494.

obvious even to the Government, but the damage was done. The trend of enlistment showed a fairly steady downward curve from about 30,000 a month in January, 1916, to under 5,000 a month in April 1917.[25]

Measures had to be adopted to check this trend. Drastic solutions were suggested and tried. A semi-active militia force was to replace all soldiers in Canada who were willing to go overseas; a board of national service directors was appointed to advise the Government and local authorities on recruiting matters and stimulate enlistment in all parts of Canada. An Order in Council was passed prohibiting all male persons between the ages of 18 and 45 from leaving Canada subject to regulations. An income tax was introduced and profit taxes were slightly increased. The formation of a French-Canadian brigade was given serious consideration—two years too late. Major-General Lessard and Colonel Blondin were sent to work up a recruiting campaign in Quebec, while members of the cabinet toured other parts of Canada in the interests of recruiting. Distinguished French veterans were sent from France to help the campaign in Quebec; and the help of the Catholic clergy from France was offered and accepted. But enlistments dropped to 3,000 in August, 1917. This was not enough to keep even two divisions in the field. The obvious answer to this manpower problem was conscription. Almost every country was using it and using it effectively. Selective conscription they found to be more efficient and more just than voluntary recruiting.

It would appear, then, that the consequent Military Service Act could have played a dual role in the Government's plans; it did help to win an election and it was also required as a most necessary spur to the war effort. Probably both of these roles were incentives to its adoption, but it is quite evident that the political potential of this move, if it was actually recognized, was vastly underrated. In fact, when the Conservatives introduced the Military Service Bill they were not at all certain that it would get the support of the majority of the country. They were afraid to trust it to a referendum, for they saw what had happened in Australia. The restrictive franchise laws are probably the best indication of the Government's lack of confidence in conscription as a vote-getter. Of course, once the election campaign was well under way there was little doubt on either side

[25]Enlistment figures have been compiled from several excerpts from *House of Commons Debates*, notably 1917, III, 2202, 2892. A full set of enlistment statistics month by month is available in the War Service Records Office of the Department of Veterans Affairs.

as to popular opinion. Outside the province of Quebec 20 anti-conscription and 150 pro-conscription members were elected to the House of Commons; the popular vote outside Quebec was 509,940 against the Government out of 1.501.719 votes cast.[26]

Conscription was not introduced specifically to win an election; for at the time of its introduction a wartime election was no certainty. Many Conservatives were vigorously urging Borden to have the life of Parliament further extended. The British government was approached through Perley to see if an extension would be granted on an address of Parliament passed by a mere party majority, and the answer was favourable.[27] Moreover, Sir Robert certainly did not see compulsory recruitment as a political stepping-stone, for having introduced the measure, he offered to resign in favour of anyone who could form a coalition government. In fact, there were men who apparently sacrificed all their political achievements in backing this measure, men such as Fielding and Graham. On the other hand, it seems no less apparent that the Borden Government did not envisage the long-term effects of conscription on the fortunes of the Conservative party. In any case one might doubt that such a realization would have swayed them from this measure. Assuredly, men on both sides of the question were most sincere.

There seems to be no proof, in short, that the leaders of the Conservative party saw conscription as a political expedient, while there is some evidence to show that the Military Service Act was introduced with fear as to its political effect. It is difficult to believe, however, that the Government was so far out of touch with popular feeling that it introduced the Act without at least a strong hope that the measure would improve the political outlook.

Quite apart from its possible implications for the Conservative party the passing of conscription seemed to be fraught with serious consequences to the country. Apparently the most serious danger was that conscription would cause a grave rift between Quebec and the rest of Canada. Conscription was opposed by a large group in Canada. Their argument that the Government had mismanaged recruiting and other military matters was undoubtedly sound, but this would not help to rectify the current serious crisis. They also maintained that conscription would split the country and that a divided country could not put forward as great an effort as a united country. This was one of the most prevalent but also one of the weakest arguments, for the country was in fact no longer united and it would become more severely rent whether conscription was introduced or no. The English-speaking provinces were growing ever more furious and indignant at Quebec, while Quebec became more bitter. Dark threats were uttered as to how Quebec would react to conscription, yet there was no guarantee that inflamed feelings in the other provinces might not also boil over. Borden wrote to Archbishop Bruchési:

Believe me, I have given much anxious thought to the consequences which you apprehend as probable or even inevitable upon the enactment of the proposed legislation. . . . But I fear your Grace may not be well informed as to the strength of feeling which exists in practically every province outside of Quebec on this question. . . . If the measure were abandoned or if no such measure had been introduced and the present Government should persist in attempting to carry on the affairs of the country in the face of so intense and vehement a feeling, disorders as grave perhaps even graver than those which your Grace apprehends would be extremely probable if not inevitable.[28]

There is a good deal to support this statement. Dafoe, for instance, a normally level-headed man, showed his intensity of feeling in a letter to Thomas Coté:

Do you not know my dear Coté, that in Australia, 14 percent of the whole population enlisted voluntarily? On that basis there would be in the Canadian armies today about 150,000 French Canadians in place of 15,000 or 20,000 at the outside. When you have done half as much as Australia it will be time for you to talk.

The trouble between the English and French Canadians has become acute, because French Canadians have refused to play their part in this war—being the only known race of white men to quit. They try to excuse themselves by alleging that they have domestic grievances which should first be righted. The excuse, if true, would be contemptible. In the face of an emergency like this domestic questions have to stand.

Do not flatter yourself with the idea that the English Canadians are disturbed by your attitude of injured innocence or your threats of reprisals. You can do precisely as you please; and we shall do whatever may be necessary. When we demonstrate, as we shall, that a solid Quebec is without power, there may be a return to reason along the banks of the St. Lawrence.[29]

One of the most moderate of the English magazines, *Saturday Night*, a pro-Laurier publication almost to the last, burst out in its turn: "Any measure taken by the Government whereby the various Provinces can be forced to give their per capita proportion toward

[28]Borden Papers, Memoir Notes, 2119.
[29]Dafoe Papers, J. W. Dafoe to Thos. Coté, Jan. 1, 1918.

the Army and to other war activities, would not only silence this nest of traitors by giving them some real work to do, but it would have the unqualified approval of Canadians from Halifax to Vancouver."[30] Or again: "There is no doubt in the world that a conspiracy exists against it [Military Service Act] in the French portions of the Province of Quebec. It is certainly not the intention of English Canada to stand idly by and see itself bled of men in order that the Quebec shirker may sidestep his responsibilities. If this maladministration of a law of the land is allowed to continue, the Government may just as well understand now as later that English Canada does not propose to put up with it."[31]

Other papers were considerably more rabid;[32] while a high ranking soldier wrote from overseas: "It seems to me that the issue of conscription now before the people will clear the air generally. If it is not decided by peaceful means I should think one day guns will have to decide that too."[33]

Nor was Borden idly prating when he spoke of the hardened veterans of Ypres, the Somme, Vimy Ridge, and Courcelette: "If what are left of 400,000 such men come back to Canada with fierce resentment in their hearts, conscious that they have been deserted and betrayed, how shall we meet them when they ask the reason? I am not so much concerned for the day when this Bill becomes law, as for the day when these men return if it is rejected."[34] How these men felt can be seen in the way they cast their ballots in December, 1917. There was only one issue for the soldier in that election and the result was almost 12 to 1 in favour of conscription.[35] Anyone who has spoken to veterans of the First World War could hardly doubt their feelings on this subject. That they could act in unison to demonstrate their purpose they showed in 1919 in Witley and Rhyll Camps. And there they were only venting minor grievances.

Despite the variety of evidence, the intensity of feeling among English-speaking Canadians on conscription has been generally disregarded by historians. One reason for this is that the English-speaking provinces were not united on the desirability of conscription whereas Quebec showed a solid front against it. Another

[30]Saturday Night, May 19, 1917.
[31]Ibid., Dec. 1, 1917; also June 9, 1917, Jan. 26, 1918, April 13, 1918, Aug. 11, 1917, Sept. 8, 1917.
[32]E. H. Armstrong, The Crisis of Quebec, 207–8.
[33]Rowell Papers, J. M. Macdonnell to Rowell, June 14, 1917.
[34]House of Commons Debates, 1917, III.
[35]Soldier votes were 215,849 for Union Government, 18,522 against: Canadian Annual Review, 1917, 643.

reason is that until the election campaign of 1917 leadership was lacking for the pro-conscription forces; but then it emerged in great strength.

Most historians also seem to have accepted the thesis that conscription was a failure, that it did not produce worthwhile results. But this is not true. The Military Service Act was passed to enlist men as required; the first requirement was repeatedly announced as being from 50,000 to 100,000 men, and the Act itself provided that "unless further authorized by Parliament the reinforcements provided under this Act shall not exceed one hundred thousand men." Conscription produced that number. The figures from different sources vary from less than 80,000 to over 170,000. The one generally accepted is 83,355 but this figure is generally conceded to be that of the number of draftees actually "on parade." This fails to take into account several categories of men who had also been raised. They were the men discharged, those whose medical category was lowered after enlistment, those on compassionate or harvest leave, and those who had enlisted in the Imperial forces. Except for harvest leave these were the types of casualties quite common to the C.E.F. before the Military Service Act, and therefore in comparing the results of conscription with those of voluntary recruitment most of them should be included. The most detailed figures available appear in the report of the Director of the Military Service Branch to his Minister in 1919.[36] They are as follows:

Made available for military service by M.S.A.		179,933
Not processed by Nov. 11	26,225	
Defaulters	24,139	
"Placed in uniform" by the M.S.A.		129,569
Of these 7,673 enlisted in Imperial forces		

The total enlistment of Canadians in the First World War is constantly quoted as 619,636. This total was arrived at by counting personnel documents or attestation papers. Out of this total 121,896 must be credited to the Military Service Act, for whether men were on leave or discharged their attestation papers remained on file. In other words:

$$\frac{M.S.A.}{\text{total enlistment}} = \frac{121,896}{619,636}$$

Reduce one figure and you must reduce the other. Neither the figure 121,896 nor 129,569 shows the effective result of conscription. Owing

[36]Canada, Sessional Papers, no. 246, 1919, "The Report of the Director of the Military Service Act to the Minister of Justice."

to circumstances only a fraction of these numbers had any influence on the outcome of the war, but what these figures represent is the total of Canadian attestations under the Act and the total of Canadian plus Imperial attestations. The figures released by the Department of National Defence are invariably lower than this: thus in the departmental memoranda of 1918 and 1919 the figure 83,355 is insisted on, with the stipulation that this does not include those discharged or on leave without pay. The total enlistments according to these memoranda is 549,339 and not 619,636.[37] The latter figure is vouched for by the machine card operators who checked these totals for the Department of Veterans Affairs. A fairly detailed study of the Military Service Act by the Historical Section of the Department of National Defence uses the figures as quoted from the Report of the Director of the Military Service Act.[38]

In any case, the monthly enlistment was raised from 4,500 in December, 1917, to over 19,000 in January, 1918, while the average enlistment for the first eight months of 1918, until the war had been virtually won, was over 18,000 a month, whereas the average monthly enlistment during 1917 had been less than 6,000. The total enlistment in the C.E.F., both draftees and volunteers, for the period the Act was in force to the end of the war was 156,018.[39] Plainly, the Military Service Act was not a failure and it was not ineffective, even though the administration of it was inefficient.

In this last respect, it proposed to fulfil its original purpose of enlisting 100,000 men by calling up selected groups as they were required. The Act divided the manhood of Canada into six classes. Class 1, to be called first, included single men age 20 to 34; these were over 400,000 in number. But the exemptions were too generous and too vague: "if it is in the national interest" was the phrase used in the Act to justify exemption. Well might an Opposition member exclaim: "By this act all may be called, and by this act all may be exempted."[40] The exemption clause was manipulated somewhat obviously for election purposes. On December 3, 1917, ten days before the election, the Government exempted all farmers from compulsory enlistment. This gave the farmers an idle winter; but then in the middle of April, when the farmers were beginning their spring work, all exemptions for the ages 20 to 22

[37]*Memoranda Respecting Work of the Department of Militia and Defence,* nos. 5 and 6, 1918 and 1919.

[38]*Memo and Statistics,* compiled by Historical Section of Department of National Defence, Nov., 1944.

[39]Month-by-month enlistment statistics at War Service Records, DVA, Ottawa.

[40]*House of Commons Debates,* 1917, IV, 3207.

were cancelled. Moreover, while the Act became law on August 29, 1917, the first men were not called until October 13, and they were not called to report until January, 1918. Undoubtedly there must be administrative lapses, but this particular lapse was not entirely in tone with the Government's grim picture of the existing crisis.

The Military Service Act, however, was to produce manpower not only for immediate reinforcements but also for the big allied effort which was envisaged, and which like the Normandy invasion of 1944 turned out to be not as costly as forecast. Accordingly, as late as September, 1918, Borden warned Lloyd George about the commitment of these reserves: "Having regard to policy practically settled before my departure as to conserving troops for decisive offensive next year I conclude that different policy has been adopted. . . . Is there any apprehension that enemy is holding powerful reserves of highly trained troops for counter attack at opportune moment. . . ."[41] The allies expected to make their big push in 1919. Fortunately the enemy broke sooner, and under the skilful leadership of Foch the allies exploited the break-through most successfully. This early victory was not foreseen by even the most sanguine in 1917 or 1918. Under these circumstances only 47,509[42] draftees were sent overseas. There are no figures to show how many of them served at the front.

Conscription in 1917–18 was one of the big issues of Canadian political life, and it continues to reappear at intervals, its advocates parading its economy, its efficiency, and its justice. But the politician shudders at its appearance and quickly turns his back. If he were induced to discuss it, he would probably admit that in the First World War conscription proved a very successful short-term political device, though its success was not foreseen. He would also have to admit that Canada's war effort, especially in manpower, compared unfavourably with that of the other major allies and with the efforts of the other Dominions; that voluntary recruiting for various reasons was dead while conscription was undoubtedly the most sensible as well as the most expedient substitute; and that Canada was fighting a war which would certainly have been lost in the spring of 1918 if other countries had followed Canada's tardy example. He probably would require some convincing that conscription did little to aggravate an existing schism; that it aired a festering issue and perhaps prevented a more serious breach. And he would then conclude: "Let's forget it. It's bad business."

[41]Perley Papers, Borden to Lloyd George, Sept. 7, 1918.
[42]*Canadian Annual Review*, 1919, 24.

Dafoe, Laurier, and the Formation of Union Government

RAMSAY COOK

THE ISSUES SURROUNDING THE ENACTMENT OF CONSCRIPTION and the formation of Union government are among the most contentious in recent Canadian history. On the one hand these events may be seen as a superb patriotic effort to assist Great Britain in the winning of the Great War. A variation of this view might characterize them as colonial Canada's reply to the call for assistance from imperial Britain. On the other hand they can, and have been interpreted as a plot on the part of scheming anti-Quebec politicians to preserve their slipping hold on office. As a sidelight to this main charge the suggestion has been made that the central objective of the promoters of Union government was to produce an administration sympathetic to the sagging fortunes of the Grand Trunk and Canadian Northern Railways. Also the suspicion has sometimes been raised that Union government was part of a plan to re-organize the British empire on a centralized basis. A final comment that is frequently made about the Unionist movement is that it destroyed that national unity which had been so carefully built, brick by brick, by Sir Wilfrid Laurier during his fifteen years of office. All of these suggestions were made in a variety of ways in 1917 and have been given some standing in the official life of Laurier, written by O. D. Skelton in 1922 while the issues were still hot. As yet, however, no thorough study has been made of the available contemporary evidence in an attempt to place together all the pieces in the enormous puzzle.

A survey of the events from the outbreak of war in August, 1914, to the election of 1917 as seen through the eyes of J. W. Dafoe suggests that the complete explanation for the support which the Unionist movement won has not yet been offered. It also suggests that much that has been written about conscription, Union government, and the

Reprinted from *Canadian Historical Review*, XLII (3), September, 1961 racial rupture of 1917 has been taken at face value from the contentions of Sir Wilfrid Laurier and his followers. Laurier was undoubtedly a most attractive figure, but he was also a practising politician—"a man who had affinities with Machiavelli as well as Sir Galahad," as Dafoe once wrote. Therefore his views are those of a man deeply engaged in political warfare; they are also only one side of the story.

Some of the details of the Unionist side can be learned by following the course which led John Dafoe to a complete break with Laurier after twenty-five years of close association. To do so requires consideration of several problems which on the surface seem to have only a tenuous connection with the disruption of 1917. These include some excursions into the tangled maze of Manitoba politics and, more particularly, a discussion of that well-worn theme—the French-language controversy in Manitoba and Ontario. These questions played an important part in destroying that unity of purpose which had characterized the country's attitude at the outset of the war. An analysis of Dafoe's attitude to these events, as well as to the critical problems of the latter half of 1917, not only helps to explain the shattering of the Laurier Liberal party, but also suggests that Canadian nationalism has more subtleties than it is sometimes allowed by Canadian historians.

As the European crisis came to a head in the late summer of 1914, John Dafoe, like most Manitobans, was giving his undivided attention to the provincial election campaign which was just drawing to a close. The *Free Press* editor, though he had always prided himself on a more than provincial interest in international affairs, was thus caught off his balance when he learned that a European war was virtually inevitable. At first he warned his readers to remain calm and wait upon events. But he left no doubt that, "If Great Britain is involved in war either by her own decision that the circumstances leave no option, or through the aggression of an outside party, it is quite certain that Canada will come to her assistance with all the power at her disposal."[1] Two days later *Free Press* subscribers were told that the Rubicon had been crossed and the issues clarified: "Upon the issue of the conflict depends the future of the Empire and the freedom of the world."[2] On August 6, the morning edition carried the terrible message on its front page, "Canada In State of War for First Time Since Becoming a Nation."[3] Thus, from the outset, the Great War was Canada's war.

Once it became clear that Great Britain was involved in war, Dafoe never wavered from the position that it was Canada's duty to become

---

[1]*Manitoba Free Press*, Aug. 3, 1914.
[2]*Ibid.*, Aug. 5, 1914.
[3]*Ibid.*, Aug. 6, 1914.

an active participant. Canadian involvement in the war, however, was not that of a colony assisting the mother country, but rather of partner nations united together in defence of a cause which in Dafoe's eyes was greater than the empire—the cause of freedom and democracy.[4] Since Canada was a full-fledged participant in the struggle for the preservation of democracy and not a mere supporting actor, the country had to be prepared to give of its blood and treasure in unstinted measure. This was made clear when the *Free Press* announced that "Whatever good things have come out of Germany it has given the world no democratic impulse. The victory of the Allies, and it must come at whatever cost and at whatever sacrifice, will feed anew the rivers of democracy flooding weary lands thirsting for freedom."[5] Sweeping aside the legal technicalities, Dafoe was convinced that Canada entered the war as a nation fighting for cherished values. Canada was one of the Allies.

At the outset of the conflict, of course, few Canadians stopped to underline this distinction. It was a measure of Dafoe's nationalism that he made it. The country, for whatever reasons, was united in its acceptance of participation in the war, and few suspected that the struggle would be of such duration as to demand that Canada exert the "totality of its powers."[6] Without stopping to ask exact definition of words or to interpret subtle nuances of phrase the vast majority of Canadians must have accepted the claim of the *Free Press* that the co-operation of the Dominions in the war effort justified the shape the empire had taken:

All the world knows that Canada, like the other self-governing Dominions, has gone into this war with the determination to fight shoulder to shoulder with Great Britain to the finish, under no compulsion save that of conscience and duty and devotion to the ideals of civilization of which the British flag is the symbol.[7]

This was an expression of responsible nationalism, not of sycophantic colonialism or aggressive imperialism. Canada was not fighting for Great Britain; she was fighting "shoulder to shoulder" with Britain and the other self-governing members of the empire.

Since Canada was engaged in a war abroad, it seemed reasonable to Dafoe that a political truce should be signed at home. He hoped it could be achieved, but his scepticism was apparent when he wrote in the first days of the war that "Sir Robert Borden at this juncture is entitled to the co-operation, sympathy and support of the Liberal party in Parliament. This he will get if he can keep Mr. Rogers and his news-

[4]*Ibid.*, Aug. 8, 1914.
[5]*Ibid.*, Sept. 7, 1914.
[6]J. W. Dafoe, *Sir Clifford Sifton in Relation to His Times* (Toronto, 1931), 406.
[7]*Manitoba Free Press*, Sept. 19, 1914.

paper echoes in hand."[8] He warned the Liberals that their duty was to give unflinching support to every proposal to forward the war effort.[9] Nevertheless he was aware that there were stirrings in the political atmosphere, especially in the Conservative party, to keep controversy alive and bring on an election in the tense war situation. Borden's Minister of Public Works, Robert Rogers, was the leading suspect. The *Free Press* argued that there should be a complete retreat from party government in the normal sense during the crisis and roundly attacked anyone suspected of fomenting dissension during the first months of the war.[10]

Both Liberals and Conservatives were conscious of the election possibilities created by the war. In December, 1914, Laurier wrote to Dafoe warning him that although the first wartime session of parliament had not ended in the expected dissolution, an early session in 1915 might be followed by an appeal to the country. He underlined the importance of "going ahead with our preparations."[11] Similar thoughts were running through the minds of prominent Conservatives.[12] Dafoe wanted to prevent both parties from disrupting the war effort for political ends. Throughout 1915 the *Free Press* repeatedly warned about the perils of partisanship. In mid-1915 a somewhat vague proposal for a coalition government was made.[13] As the constitutional limit on Parliament's duration drew nearer fears increased in Dafoe's mind that the Liberals, seeing an advantage in the growing weaknesses of the Conservatives, might force an election.[14] The *Free Press* argued that an election should be prevented by an extension of the life of the existing Parliament[15] and expressed enthusiastic approval when the parties agreed to take this step.[16]

The truce advocated by the *Free Press* during the first two years of the war did not mean that the paper was uncritical of the Government's military programme. But it did drop much of its partisan tone when dealing with national politics. When the paper criticized the Borden administration it was usually for not doing enough. Repeatedly Dafoe's paper demanded a more active recruiting campaign.[17] But

[8]*Ibid.*, Aug. 6, 1914.
[9]*Ibid.*, Nov. 16, 1914.
[10]*Ibid.*, Oct. 10, 12, 20, 1914.
[11]Public Archives of Canada (henceforth P.A.C.), Dafoe Papers, Laurier to Dafoe, Dec. 16, 1914.
[12]P.A.C., Willison Papers, Sir John Willison to Sir Edward Kemp, May 5, 1915.
[13]*Manitoba Free Press*, May 12, 1915.
[14]*Ibid.*, Dec. 6, 1915.
[15]*Ibid.*, Dec. 30, 1915.
[16]*Ibid.*, Feb. 10, 1916.
[17]*Ibid.*, Oct. 14, 1914; Nov. 13, 1914; Nov. 20, 1914.

politics in the partisan sense were largely banished from the newspaper's comments on the federal Government.

In Manitoba a different situation obtained. Dafoe's *Free Press* had long been the bitterest critic of Sir Rodmond Roblin's Conservative government. Therefore the cessation of political asperities on the national front never tempted Dafoe to adopt a similar attitude toward the local Conservatives. This fact boded ill for the continuance of national political peace because of the close connection between the Manitoba Premier and his former colleague, Robert Rogers, federal Minister of Public Works.[18] It is thus somewhat ironic that the demission of Roblin's government in May, 1915, rather than contributing to political peace, led directly to new disturbances which spilled over into federal politics and set the stage for the destruction of the unity of the Liberal party. The source of this new friction was the ever irritable school question which cut across party lines and threatened the nation's unity. With the Liberal party finally in power in Manitoba, Dafoe grasped the opportunity to press for long advocated educational reforms. These reforms demanded the removal of the multiplicity of languages from Manitoba schools, and their replacement by English. For Dafoe this was necessary not simply for educational reasons, but also for national reasons. The common school was to be made the effective agency of the Canadian *Kulturkampf*. "Our gates are open to the oppressed of Europe," the *Free Press* explained, "but when they come here they must forget their feuds, forswear their racial aspirations, and become Canadians not only in name but in fact."[19] The new Liberal administration agreed essentially with the *Free Press* view that all non-English privileges, including the meagre rights that had been allowed to the French Canadians after 1897, should be removed from Manitoba's educational structure. After a quarter of a century of controversy Manitoba schools were thus transformed into exclusively English language institutions.[20] But the controversy was by no means concluded.

The educational reforms in Manitoba coincided with the growing agitation being carried on by the French-Canadian leaders in Ontario against less radical changes brought about by the famous Regulation 17. Clearly there was a serious racial fracas boiling up in the early months of 1916. The question of bilingual schools was not one that could be easily kept within the confines of Manitoba and Ontario, for the province of Quebec naturally felt that its interests were at stake.

18*Ibid.*, June 3, 1915.
19*Ibid.*, Aug. 10, 1914.
20W. L. Morton, *Manitoba: A History* (Toronto, 1957), 352.

Thus, the eruption of the question into national politics was all but inevitable. That this should happen when the war was entering a new and serious phase and the manpower situation was beginning to evoke incriminating glances at the French Canadians only increased the explosiveness of the language issue. In the early months of 1916 Laurier consulted with his provincial leaders in both Manitoba and Ontario in an effort to encourage their opposition to any limitations that might be placed upon French-language rights in the provinces.[21] The Conservative party was also feeling the pressure of racial tensions. Prime Minister Borden was faced with a revolt on the part of his French-Canadian ministers who threatened to absent themselves from Cabinet meetings until some action was taken by the federal authorities to ensure that the French-language privileges would be respected by the provinces.[22] While Borden was able to adopt the position that the federal government could not interfere in the provinces' control of educational matters,[23] Laurier was faced with a more threatening situation. His claim to the leadership of his people was at stake. In April, 1916, he began considering the introduction of a resolution into the federal parliament requesting the province of Ontario to recognize the French-language rights.[24] Over the opposition of provincial lieutenants and federal advisers[25] he decided to take the dangerous step. The carefully phrased Lapointe resolution came before the House of Commons on May 9, 1916.[26] Moderate though the resolution was, the intensity of feeling evoked by the war was allowed full vent in the subsequent debate. Though the resolution referred specifically to Ontario, it interested Canadians everywhere, especially in Manitoba.

The question raised by the Lapointe resolution was of that rare category which may cause even the most ardent partisan to sunder his party allegiance. John Dafoe was convinced that Laurier had committed the gravest error in introducing into federal politics a question that belonged only in the provincial arena. Naturally his conviction was strengthened by the belief that Ontario and Manitoba had acted correctly in their educational reforms. He was prepared therefore to place his convictions above his loyalty to Laurier—a loyalty which had never been blind. He expressed his conviction to an old French-Canadian friend who accused him of fathering the new Manitoba

[21]P.A.C., Laurier Papers, Laurier to T. C. Norris, Feb. 22, 1916; Laurier to N. W. Rowell, March 1, 1916.

[22]P.A.C., Borden Papers, T. C. Casgrain, P. E. Blondin, E. L. Patinaude to Borden, April 20, 1916.

[23]Ibid., Borden to T. C. Casgrain, P. E. Blondin, E. L. Patinaude, April 24, 1916.

[24]Laurier Papers, L. O. David to Laurier, April 15, 1916.

[25]Ibid., N. W. Rowell to Laurier, April 15, 1916; W. S. Fielding to Laurier, April 23, 1916.

[26]Wade, Mason, *The French Canadians* (New York, 1955), 696.

school legislation and warned him that he had "brought into the world a child who has all the appearances of a monster."[27] Dafoe's rejoinder was that he was only one of a number of parents who had come to see that the "absurd arrangement arrived at in 1897" could no longer be allowed to exist "if the province of Manitoba was not to be transformed into middle Europe on a small scale." Of course, the French might have been given special consideration, but the obvious fact was that their leaders, especially the clergy, intended to use their privileges to transform the schools into clerical institutions, thus destroying the willingness of Manitobans to give them preferential treatment. If the French acted in a reasonable manner they would probably be given fair treatment, Dafoe asserted, but the province had no intention of being intimidated by the people of Quebec "who appear to think they have a right to impose their will throughout the length and breadth of Canada." This delusion was the belief of Henri Bourassa and the Quebec Liberals had succumbed to his influence. He continued with evident heat:

> I know that you boast that you have beaten Bourassa and put him out of business; but as a matter of fact he has conquered you. He may not command your allegiance but he controls your minds. You all think his thoughts, talk his language, echo his threats; and I should suspect that when Sir Wilfrid Laurier passes away—may that day be long distant—that you will accept him as your chief.[28]

The suggestion that the French Canadians were entitled to equal rights throughout the Dominion sparked from Dafoe a further exposition of his growing suspicion that the Liberal party was falling under the long shadow of Henri Bourassa. The acceptance of Bourassa's views could only lead to the formation of political parties on racial lines. "I should be sorry to see anything like this happen," he concluded darkly, "but I have no doubt that this will happen if the Nationalist movement in Quebec becomes more formidable than it is, and swallows up both the Liberal and Conservative parties as it gives promise of doing."[29]

Prior to the Lapointe resolution Dafoe had publicly warned the Liberal party of the danger of countenancing any federal interference in the provinces' educational affairs.[30] Early in May he travelled to Ottawa to exert his personal influence directly with the party leadership. He talked with Laurier and found him "stubborn as an army mule." As Dafoe saw matters, the party was inextricably caught on the horns of a dilemma. "If the whole party follows Laurier, the party is

27Dafoe Papers, Thomas Coté to Dafoe, March 27, 1916.
28Ibid., Dafoe to Thomas Coté, April 6, 1916.
29Ibid., April 17, 1916.
30Manitoba Free Press, April 15, 1916.

gone; if the French follow him, Laurier is gone as a national leader."[31] Sir Clifford Sifton was outraged at Laurier's attitude. In his characteristic, downright way he described the Liberal leader as acting "the part of a boy who has just been elected for a back concession and thinks that he will not be elected again unless he shouts for his county." The sooner the party was rid of him, the better for the entire country.[32] But where Dafoe was unsuccessful in influencing Laurier, he was in a stronger position with the western Liberal members. Apart from their personal views they were fully aware of the weight that the *Manitoba Free Press* carried in their "back concessions." Dafoe's influence was therefore important in producing the split which divided the Liberal party when the roll call on the Lapointe resolution was taken.[33] Eleven western Liberals and one from Ontario kicked over the party traces and opposed the passage of the resolution.[34] The rupture of national unity and the beginning of western severance of its loyalty to the Liberal party were thus the two most important consequences of the debate on the school controversy in the federal parliament in the spring of 1916. Both Laurier and Dafoe, in their separate ways, were responsible for these developments: Laurier because he had approved the tactics of the Lapointe resolution, Dafoe because he had encouraged the western Liberals to break with their leader.

Even before the episode of the Lapointe resolution Dafoe had come to the conclusion that the majority of the Quebec leaders had fallen under the spell of Bourassa, but he had not yet placed Laurier under this condemnation. By May, 1916, however, he was no longer sure that Laurier was uncontaminated. In the *Free Press* he placed the responsibility for the Lapointe resolution squarely on Laurier's shoulders. Moreover he made it clear that "there will be no yielding at any point to these Nationalist demands, which have so unaccountably received the blessing of the French Liberal chiefs."[35] Everywhere but in Quebec, where the Liberals were already too strong, the result of the foolhardy Lapointe resolution would be a serious weakening of the party. In the West, only the Laurier Liberals would suffer, for the western Liberals had issued their declaration of independence. This action should be followed by the formation of a radical, progressive western Liberal party, the *Free Press* advised. In contrast to the exist-

---

[31]P.A.C., Sifton Papers, Dafoe to Sifton, May 7, 1916.

[32]Dafoe Papers, Sifton to Dafoe, May 11, 1916.

[33]J. W. Dafoe, *Laurier: A Study in Canadian Politics* (Toronto, 1922), 161–2.

[34]O. D. Skelton, *The Life and Letters of Sir Wilfrid Laurier* (2 vols., London, 1922), II, 488.

[35]*Manitoba Free Press*, May 12, 1916.

ing parties the members of the new group "will be far more interested in furthering their programme than in office-holding and will be indifferent to the time-servers and opportunists to whom the enjoyment of office is the be-all and end-all of political existence. 'To Your Tents, O Israel!' "[36]

Thus the Lapointe resolution can be seen as the first tremor in an approaching earthquake in Canadian politics. The language question had been aired and set aside, but firm positions had been occupied and French and English in Canada now peered across a gulf at one another through spectacles smeared with renewed distrust. The tremor seriously shook Dafoe's faith in the Liberal leadership. He had disagreed with Laurier in a more fundamental way than ever before, and this time the western Liberal members had followed his teachings. Though he was not ready to break finally with Laurier yet, he no longer trusted the old man.

Dafoe's distrust of Laurier increased his anxiety to prevent ·an election. The country was in a state of turmoil and opposition to the Borden government was growing increasingly apparent. It was possible that the benefit of this discontent might not accrue to the Liberals, but even if it did, Dafoe was not anxious to see them returned to power. If Laurier, back in office, surrounded himself with the old guard, no advance on the existing government's hesitant leadership could be expected. Dafoe offered these reflections to Sifton and concluded by pointing out that there was one possibility that would require careful watching:

I have some reason to believe that some very daring spirits in the Conservative party are trying to induce the Government to adopt conscription for the purpose of bringing the trouble in Quebec to a head with a view to a dissolution at that particular moment. So daring a stroke might save the Government, with the consequences that the domestic peace of Canada might be threatened.[37]

Perhaps that was just another of those rumours that frequently circulated in political smoking rooms, but it suggested that Canadian politics were entering a profoundly unsettled state. The disruption created by the French-language question and the increasingly frequent criticisms that were being directed at the Borden administration edged open the flood gates through which began to flow the currents of renewed political strife.

Dafoe's declining confidence in Laurier's leadership in the spring of 1916 was not coupled with any growing attraction to the existing Conservative government. He was disturbed by the repeated charges of

[36]*Ibid.*, May 13, 1916.
[37]Sifton Papers, Dafoe to Sifton, Oct. 17, 1916.

corruption in the Conservative direction of the war effort and felt justified in encouraging a vigilant Opposition.[38] But more disquieting than the evidence of corruption was the critical manpower situation. If the war was to be fought to a decisive conclusion Canada and her allies had to keep their military strength at full capacity. Premier Borden recognized that necessity when, in January, 1916, he called for an increase in Canada's forces to 500,000 men. This objective, which was to be achieved by voluntary enlistment, had the full support of the *Free Press*.[39] But before the end of 1916 it was obvious to anyone with eyes to see that the necessary men could not be obtained by voluntary means. For a variety of reasons, including Government blundering, the stream of enlistments had dwindled to a trickle.[40] What could be done to meet this critical situation? In April, 1916, the *Free Press* expressed the view that conscription, at least under a party government, would lack the necessary support of a united public.[41] But was there any alternative to conscription?

During the summer of 1916 Dafoe began to move toward a possible solution to the combined political and manpower problem. One thing was patently clear—the existing leadership had failed.[42] In December, 1916, the *Free Press* offered its readers a depressing appraisal of the country's political situation:

> We have had during the war a mean-spirited, selfish, far from competent, patronage-dispensing Government, made up in large part of inveterate and embittered partisans, whose first thought is for themselves and their positions and the jobs and patronage they can deliver to their supporters. . . .
> The Liberal opposition has retaliated, as was inevitable, with the consequence that we have not a united people intent upon the greatest task that ever fell to our nation, but a country distracted by partisan strife, drifting surely and steadily into a General Election which will still further divide the people into warring factions.[43]

But even as he was writing these lines Dafoe was working out a solution which he hoped would save the country from renewed political conflict and provide the leadership necessary to prevent the war effort from slowing to a halt. He was convinced that the chief members of the Borden government, led by Robert Rogers, were corruptionists. The Prime Minister himself was "a well meaning incompetent." But the Liberals were no better. "No Liberal Government made up of the

[38]*Manitoba Free Press*, April 12, 1916.
[39]*Ibid.*, April 14, 1916.
[40]A. M. Willms, "Conscription 1917: A Brief for the Defence," *C.H.R.*, XXXVII, 4 (Dec. 1956), 342–5.
[41]*Manitoba Free Press*, April 17, 1916.
[42]*Ibid.*, Oct. 4, 1916.
[43]*Ibid.*, Dec. 20, 1916.

public men in sight could give the people of Canada what they want: a leadership so plainly disinterested and competent as to command their whole-hearted support," he wrote confidently. Since an electoral duel between the existing party leaders could produce no satisfactory result and would only divide the country, it'had to be avoided. One possibility would be to replace half the existing cabinet with Conservative businessmen like Augustus Nanton, the two Galts, and Sir Joseph Flavelle. The other possibility was a coalition between the Liberals and the Conservatives. Canadian history offered an encouraging parallel. Dafoe hardly needed to remind G. M. Wrong that, "If Brown and Macdonald could sink their differences—personal and political—to bring about Confederation, Sir Wilfrid and Sir Robert (between whom there is personal friendship) might be able to loyally combine for a far greater purpose."[44] Such a coalition seemed the obvious course to promote.

As the year 1917 opened Dafoe began his campaign for a union government. He admitted that the arrangement would not be easily achieved. "It will require the united effort of the nation," he argued, "to substitute a National Government for blind partisan leadership of the blind."[45] Dafoe was one of many people who were prepared to make the effort. In February of the new year he travelled to Ottawa on business. While there he took the opportunity to survey the political scene. His observations were hardly encouraging. "Both sides," he concluded, "are bent on playing the old party game with all its vigour, just as though we were not in the third year of the greatest war that has ever been seen." The Government, he suspected, wanted to maintain office for the benefit of its supporters, and hoped to force a further extension of the parliamentary term. The Opposition, believing that discontent throughout the country favoured it, was not disposed to permit any further postponement of an election. Dafoe felt certain that the Liberal interpretation was wrong; the country was equally disgusted with them, and they would suffer especially from anti-Quebec propaganda. As far as the West was concerned its sympathies were either "populist" or independent Liberal. Probably a national government, an idea which was gaining considerable support in the East, was the best solution.[46] That Dafoe's view of the situation was fairly accurate is suggested by a remark made by Sir Joseph Flavelle that the main concern of the two parties in the spring of 1917 was "How to win for the party."[47]

44Dafoe Papers, Dafoe to G. M. Wrong, Dec. 12, 1916.
45*Manitoba Free Press*, Jan. 13, 1917.
46Sifton Papers, Dafoe to Sifton, Feb. 12, 1917.
47P.A.C., Flavelle Papers, Sir Joseph Flavelle to R. H. Brand, March 14, 1917.

The Liberals were certainly preparing for an election. In April Laurier sent George Graham and E. M. MacDonald west to scout the situation. He then consulted Dafoe directly on the advisability of an election.[48] Dafoe repeated his view that although the Government was obviously in a weak position, the Liberals would be put on the defensive if they forced an appeal to the country. A Conservative defeat seemed inevitable "unless some new factor enters the contest and gives them a good battle cry," he admitted, but there were other factors to consider. The Conservatives could invoke the Quebec whipping-horse, making good use of the indiscretions of certain Quebec Liberals. Such an appeal would find much sympathy in English Canada. Perhaps hoping to discourage Laurier, he concluded with an eye to the future:

I think it very necessary in the interests of the whole country that a Liberal Government should be in office for the period immediately following the war. I don't think anything can prevent this coming about unless in some way the Liberals throw the control of the situation into the hands of the Government. They might do this by forcing an election. They ought, therefore, to be very sure that they are right before going forward.[49]

On his return from the meetings of the Imperial War Cabinet and visits to the front early in May, Sir Robert Borden threw the confused political situation into further disorder by announcing that the Government would ask parliament to adopt legislation providing for military conscription. The *Manitoba Free Press* immediately agreed that conscription was necessary, but insisted that it could not be carried out by a party government. The Canadian people would only trust a national, win-the-war government with such extensive powers.[50] On May 29 Borden proposed to Laurier that a coalition should be formed to enforce the proposed enlistment policy. On the following day Dafoe informed the Liberal leader, "I am bound to say that I think that public opinion is very strongly in favour of the formation of a National Government and the adoption of whatever policy is necessary to secure such reinforcements for our troops at the front as will prevent the gradual disappearance of our armies by wastage."[51] Laurier, however, clung to his long-standing promise to oppose conscription and refused to enter a coalition pledged to its implementation.[52]

Thus conscription came to Canada, and with it a political revolution. Laurier chose to oppose compulsory enlistment in keeping with the

[48]Laurier Papers, Laurier to Dafoe, April 10, 1917.
[49]*Ibid.*, Dafoe to Laurier, April 26, 1917.
[50]*Manitoba Free Press*, May 21, 1917.
[51]Laurier Papers, Dafoe to Laurier, May 30, 1917.
[52]Skelton, *Laurier*, II, 512–13.

promise he had made at the outset of the war. His grounds for opposition are worthy of note:

In the Province of Quebec I have been accused by the Nationalists of being a conscious or unconscious Jingoist and of leading the country to conscription. This was on account of the truth which I often proclaimed that our position in the British Empire might make it imperative for us to participate in wars in which Britain might be engaged. At the same time I asserted that this did not lead to conscription, and that I was opposed to conscription. The statement was never objected to by either friend or foe, the Nationalists excepted. If I were now to take a different attitude, I would simply hand over the Province to the Nationalists, and the consequences might be very serious.[53]

Two points should be emphasized concerning Laurier's view. First, Laurier agreed that Canada might be called upon to assist in British wars. Dafoe, and those of his stripe, saw the matter in a different light —Canada was fighting her own war in co-operation with Great Britain and the Dominions. Secondly, Laurier clearly expressed his fear that if he supported conscription he would lose the leadership of the French Canadians to Henri Bourassa. Dafoe in his study of Laurier proposed the thesis that Laurier's career after 1911 could best be understood in terms of two objectives: "to win back if he could the Prime Ministership of Canada; but in any event to establish his position forever as the unquestioned, unchallenged leader of his people." When the two objectives conflicted, Dafoe believed that Laurier invariably chose the second.[54] It has been strongly argued that Dafoe's assessment was wrong and that Laurier's decisions were always made from the point of view of what in his judgment would best preserve national unity.[55] Yet in the case of conscription it is obvious from Laurier's letter that his most acute fear during the conscription crisis was that he would lose Quebec to the Nationalists. Of course he argued that such an eventuality would jeopardize national unity. The fear was entirely justified, but it failed to take account of the fact that the majority of English Canadians supported conscription as enthusiastically as the French Canadians opposed it, as the election of December, 1917, indicated. Whatever choice Laurier, or any other politician made, national unity was threatened. Laurier quite naturally made the choice which placed him in agreement with his compatriots. Perhaps Dafoe oversimplified Laurier's motivation and failed to see that the Liberal leader was really faced with an insoluble dilemma,

[53]Laurier Papers, Laurier to A. C. Hardy, May 29, 1917.
[54]Dafoe, *Laurier*, 156–7.
[55]H. Blair Neatby, *Laurier and a Liberal Quebec*, (Unpublished Ph.D. thesis, University of Toronto, 1955), 385.

but it can hardly be doubted that Dafoe struck upon one of the primary impulses which brought Laurier to his anti-conscriptionist position.

Dafoe, of course, supported conscription, but he seriously doubted that it could be implemented successfully by a party government that had lost much of its support in the country. The *Free Press* warned of the danger of combining political partisanship with compulsory enlistment:

National unity such as Canada has scarcely known is imperative for conscription as a practical policy; the issue in its present form is already being exploited in the interests of partisan politics. The measure may be good, but the methods hitherto pursued are as bad as any methods could easily be.[56]

Both Liberals and Conservatives were exploiting conscription for political advantage, Dafoe believed. A means of preventing continued partisanship had to be found—a means, it was hoped, that would ensure the country's united support of the necessary recruiting policy.[57]

In mid-June Dafoe again journeyed to Ottawa where he had a brief, inconclusive interview with Laurier who was now suggesting that conscription should be postponed until after a national referendum.[58] Dafoe also consulted with the western Liberals with a view to having them form an independent group which could force both parties to accept a further extension of parliament. He still believed that an election was the most serious threat to national unity.[59]

Back in Winnipeg, Dafoe conducted some further tests of the political temperature. T. A. Crerar, "the big man in the farmers' movement," believed that a western bloc of Liberals and farmers should be sent to Ottawa.[60] Certainly there was little sympathy for Laurier's viewpoint. Dafoe decided that the time had now come to break completely with Laurier. Perhaps the Quebec situation would have been better if Laurier had been taken into the Government at the outset of the war, but the opportunity had been missed and the time had come to face the realities of Quebec politics. The *Free Press* gave its frank assessment.

The authentic voice of Quebec today is that of Bourassa. He has been stating his views with perfect frankness. He says Quebec is against the war. Laurier is at best a moderating, not a controlling power in Quebec. If he came into a coalition government he would leave Quebec behind him. This is why the problem now before the people of Canada must be solved, if there is any solution, without the assistance of Laurier or Quebec.[61]

[56]*Manitoba Free Press*, June 1, 1917.
[57]*Ibid.*, June 13, 1917.
[58]Laurier Papers, Laurier to Dafoe, June 20, 1917.
[59]Dafoe, *Sifton*, 405.
[60]Dafoe Papers, Dafoe to Sifton, June 27, 1917.
[61]*Manitoba Free Press*, June 25, 1917.

The only solution, as Dafoe saw it, was a coalition government without the support of Laurier and Quebec. "Even majorities have rights in this country," the *Free Press* remarked angrily. By mid-July, 1917, the Winnipeg newspaper had read all the anti-conscriptionists out of the Liberal party.[62]

During another visit to Ottawa in early July Dafoe freely expressed his conviction that despite Laurier's refusal to join a coalition the cause of national government was far from dead. He was confident that a plan satisfactory to western leaders could be devised.[63] What was necessary was to unite all the conscriptionist forces so as to smother the Laurier Liberals. "If we can prevent a party fight in the West we shall have no trouble with the foreigners," he assured Premier Borden.[64] But the western Liberal leaders were fully aware of their own strength and were reluctant to throw their weight behind Borden. Dafoe talked with the western Liberal leaders and reported the results to N. W. Rowell, one of the chief eastern promoters of the Unionist cause:

> I could see that their preference was to fight the coming election as a Western group on the platform to be adopted next month, and after thus proving their strength to join the Conservatives in a Union Government for the balance of the war. They seemed to fear that if they went into a Union Government at present they might not carry the whole Liberal strength in Western Canada with them; whereas by the other course they thought it might be possible to keep the party intact as a factor behind the war government. You will undoubtedly recognize the point of view as not being altogether different from that held by some of the Eastern leaders.[65]

The future of the coalition movement seemed to rest with the Western Liberal Convention which was to meet in Winnipeg on August 7 to draw up a platform for the increasingly independent western wing of the Liberal party. The *Free Press* probably gauged western sentiment fairly accurately when it claimed that the West

> has no confidence in the present Dominion Government as a whole or in any member of it as an individual. It admits no allegiance either to the leaders on the other side of the House.
>
> The Canadian West is in the mood to break away from the past affiliations and traditions and inaugurate a new political era of sturdy support for advanced and radical programmes. The break up of the parties has given the West its opportunity; and there is no doubt but that it will take advantage of it.[66]

---

[62]*Ibid.*, July 7, 1917.
[63]Willison Papers, Arthur Ford to Sir John Willison, July 19, 1917.
[64]Borden Papers, Dafoe to Borden, July 18, 1917.
[65]Dafoe Papers, Dafoe to N. W. Rowell, July 25, 1917.
[66]*Manitoba Free Press*, June 28, 1917.

But even in the radical West war policies were matters of prime concern, especially the questions of conscription and coalition government.

Laurier hoped that the Winnipeg convention would confine itself to the questions of domestic politics which affected the West, but he feared that Sir Clifford Sifton would try to commit the delegates to conscription. He advised his supporters to avoid the conscription issue and follow the policy he was advocating—that of leaving conscription an open question to be settled by individual consciences.[67] Both the conscription and anti-conscription forces were manœuvring for control of the western Liberal meeting. The Laurier Liberals feared that the Siftons, Dafoe, and Calder of Saskatchewan were throwing all their influence and money behind a conscriptionist delegation.[68] The proponents of conscription, on the other hand, were suspicious that the men who controlled the party machine and especially the large foreign vote were attempting to pack the gathering with anti-conscriptionist delegates.[69]

Dafoe himself harboured doubts about the outcome of the convention. Though he realized that a large step toward a union government would be taken if the convention resolved in favour of a coalition, he thought that was too much to expect. One of the danger signals had been the Liberal Convention held in Toronto on July 20 which had expressed its full confidence in Laurier.[70] Dafoe thought that the most important problem was to see that the western Liberals were kept straight on the issue of winning the war.[71] He was greatly irritated when George P. Graham asked him to watch the convention carefully to prevent it from developing an anti-French line. In a burst of anger Dafoe retorted:

I hope most Westerners are as tired as I am of being told that we must not do this because Quebec would not like it, or that the party must do that because otherwise Quebec will rally to Bourassa. After one has been told twenty-five times in succession, as I was at Ottawa, that our national course on the war must be determined by the consideration that it is preferable that Laurier instead of Bourassa should control Quebec the dose becomes nauseating. I did for a while think this myself, but I now believe this is the wrong view.

Already, he continued, Bourassa controlled Laurier because of the latter's fear that he would lose the leadership of his people. Should

[67]Laurier Papers, Laurier to A. W. McLeod, July 31, 1917.
[68]*Ibid.*, A. W. McLeod to Laurier, July 27, 1917.
[69]Dafoe Papers, G. H. Barr to Dafoe, July 27, 1917.
[70]What appears to be an authentic account of the speeches delivered at this meeting was printed in the *Toronto Evening Telegram*, August 30, 1917, p. 16. A discussion of the genesis of this revealing document is found in Arthur R. Ford, *As The World Wags On* (Toronto, 1950), 94–5.
[71]Dafoe Papers, Dafoe to N. W. Rowell, July 25, 1917.

Laurier become premier again Bourassa would be the power behind the throne. Such a situation would be completely intolerable. Laurier, Dafoe judged, was now playing exclusively for the benefit of his people, claiming that if the English-Canadian Liberals suppressed their views, victory would be in the hands of the party. Laurier should have joined the coalition when Borden offered him the opportunity. He could have made his support conditional on the postponement of conscription until one last appeal for voluntary recruits was made by a national government. Had he taken this stand, Sir Wilfrid "would have closed his career secure in the confidence and affection certainly of the English Canadians, and I believe also of the better half of his own people."[72] Thus, for Dafoe, there was no longer any question of subordinating the issue of conscription to the exigencies of Liberal party unity.

But when the Western Liberal Convention met, Dafoe found himself in a minority with these strong views. Right from the outset it was clear that a majority of the delegates favoured continued support for Laurier and the Liberal party. On his arrival in Winnipeg at the outset of the convention, Main Johnson, who had gone West to watch the proceedings for N. W. Rowell, found Dafoe already convinced that the meeting was a Laurier gathering. After a conversation with Dafoe, Johnson, whose recently opened papers revealed a mine of information on the western meeting, made these important observations:

I believe the strength of opinion is against the Borden government rather than for Laurier, but this anti-Borden feeling, naturally enough, perhaps, is personified in his chief opponent, Laurier. There is no doubt at all of the intenseness of disgust with the present government. The delegates seem to think that to put them out is the immediate and chief patriotic duty to perform.

Dafoe pointed out the different, powerful sources from which Sir Wilfrid draws his power at the present time:—

1. The French people.
2. The Roman Catholic Church—French and English.
3. The C.P.R., the Bank of Montreal and probably the majority of the big interests.
4. The foreign vote.
5. The strong party Liberals who want to get into power and who see the chance now.

As an important factor, not fundamental, but a very proximate one, is the ill-timed visit of Sir Clifford Sifton. His unpopularity among the rank-and-file of Western Liberals seems to be unanimous, and he was here at about the time the delegates were being chosen.[73]

---

[72]*Ibid.*, Dafoe to George Graham, July 30, 1917.
[73]Toronto Public Library, Main Johnson Papers, Diary, Main Johnson to N. W. Rowell, Aug. 7, 1917.

Seeing these factors at work in the convention from the beginning, Dafoe apparently decided to try to salvage something from a desperate situation. Probably he worked through his friends, Premier Norris and A. B. Hudson, who led the Manitoba delegation. After many hours of labour in the Resolutions Committee, a compromise "Win-the-War" resolution, devised by Dafoe, was brought forward by Dr. D. B. Neely. It called for maximum war effort but eschewed any mention of conscription. Perhaps it was thought that such a resolution could be later interpreted as implying the necessity of both conscription and coalition. Unfortunately for those who hoped to profit from ambiguity, J. G. Turriff, a conscriptionist Liberal, remained unsatisfied and attempted to have the convention amend the motion to provide for compulsory military service if it became necessary. Not only was his effort a failure, but the debate revealed the sharp division within the western Liberal camp, and the strength of the anti-conscriptionist delegates.[74]

Having refused to support conscription, the convention turned to an enthusiastic and, by all reports, highly emotional endorsation of Sir Wilfrid Laurier's leadership. Nevertheless, Main Johnson felt that the resolution was only lukewarm, confining itself chiefly to Laurier's past record. Like the "Win-the-War" statement, it too was a compromise after a battle in the Resolutions Committee.[75] Thus on all major points, the convention turned thumbs down on the views that Dafoe had hoped to see accepted. As he later wrote, the meeting developed into "a bomb that went off in the hands of its makers."[76] Perhaps Dafoe accepted this result as substantiation of a rumour he had heard earlier of a bargain that had been struck between some western and Quebec Liberals: in return for western acceptance of Quebec's attitude to the war effort, French-Canadian Liberals would support western demands for tariff reform.[77] Certainly the convention was a serious defeat for the cause of Union government and conscription and a personal defeat for Dafoe and his newspaper, which had almost been openly condemned by the delegates.[78]

The machine politicians had won, the *Free Press* maintained. The West's true aspirations had been thwarted by a group of scheming politicians who cared little for the vigorous prosecution of the war.[79] But plans for a coalition government were not to be discarded so easily. Sifton, with his ardour little dampened by the set-back, proceeded to

[74]*Ibid.*, Main Johnson to N. W. Rowell, Aug. 9, 1917 (morning).
[75]*Ibid.*, Aug. 9, 1917 (afternoon).
[76]Dafoe Papers, Dafoe to A. Bridle, June 14, 1921.
[77]Main Johnson Papers, Diary, Main Johnson to N. W. Rowell, Aug. 7, 1917.
[78]Laurier Papers, J. K. Barrett to Laurier, Aug. 9, 1917.
[79]*Manitoba Free Press*, Aug. 10, 1917.

Ottawa leaving Dafoe to develop the western situation. It was well that Sifton had gone East, for Dafoe was aware that his business connections made him suspect in the West, and this unpopularity had contributed to the result of the Western Liberal Convention.[80] In Ottawa Sifton decided "to go in & fight it out to the finish."[81] For a month negotiations continued in the East with the important western leaders shuttling back and forth after being briefed by Dafoe. Dafoe's task was to persuade the westerners that the success of Union government depended upon their inclusion in it. He assured them that it was simply a war government in which no one would be expected to compromise his views on domestic policy.[82]

In mid-September the Borden government took a step which no doubt helped to convince the westerners that Union government was desirable. This step was the adoption of two new and unusual electoral laws, the Military Voters' Act and the Wartime Elections Act. The clauses of the latter Act which disfranchised "enemy aliens" were particularly important to the western politicians, for a large sector of their constituents was made up of these people. How much of a fillip this legislation gave to the Unionist cause is impossible to determine exactly; it certainly did not bring the protests from the West that some Unionists evidently expected.[83] By the first week in October the westerners were ready to throw in their lot with the coalition, and on October 12, the successful culmination of the months of critical negotiations was announced to the Canadian public.

The final act in the drama of Union government and the break-up of the Liberal party was the election which was called for December 17, 1917. For the first time since he had joined the *Free Press*, Dafoe and his newspaper were arrayed against the Liberals. Many of his life-long political friends were now his bitter foes. But Dafoe had decided months earlier that the issues of the war were far more important than political loyalties. He told his correspondent in Ottawa in October, 1917, that although he had no intention of making the *Free Press* an organ of the new government, he would give it strong independent support. No longer should Sir Wilfrid be represented as the gallant knight, for he had to be made to realize the "shameful mess" he had

[80]Dafoe Papers, Dafoe to Borden, Sept. 29, 1917. There is very wide agreement that Sifton's presence in Winnipeg worked to the advantage of the Laurier forces. See Main Johnson's letter quoted above: also, *Toronto Evening Telegram*, Aug. 7, 1917, p. 7; *Canadian Courier*, Aug. 25, 1917. A writer in the latter journal could hardly have emphasized the point more than when he wrote, ". . . the plain truth is that even "Bob" Rogers has not one tenth of the number of bitter enemies among Western Liberals as has Sir Clifford Sifton."

[81]Dafoe Papers, Sifton to Dafoe, Aug. 14, 1917.

[82]*Ibid.*, Aug. 12, 1917 (Deciphered telegram).

[83]P.A.C., Rowell Papers, N. W. Rowell to F. Pardee, Sept. 19, 1917.

made of things. Dafoe's personal view was that it would be best for the old warrior to resign, for his continued leadership could only mean the ruin of the Liberal party by identifying it with an anti-war programme.[84]

Laurier, of course, persisted courageously in the course he believed was right despite the signs that the ground was crumbling under him. In Dafoe's view there were but two alternatives before the Canadian electorate and the correct one was obvious:

> The choice is between the Government which represents, so far as the complex conditions of Canadian political life have made it possible for it to represent, every section of the community which is in favour of winning the war, and a party just as definitely pledged against the measures by which alone this Dominion's obligations and given word can be fulfilled, and which will be supported by all the elements opposed, from various motives, to the pursuit of an active war policy.[85]

In the heat of partisan strife, Dafoe identified the views of the Laurier Liberals with those of the Bourassa Nationalists, and misrepresented them both.[86]

The result was never in serious doubt. The Government, campaigning on the issue of conscription which was popular in English Canada, and with the assistance of its unusual electoral machinery, far outclassed the truncated Liberal party. At last on December 17 the unequal, but bitterly fought, winter campaign ended. The result showed the Laurier Liberals reduced to little more than a party of French Canadians, while the Unionist roster sagged under the weight of its enormous English-Canadian representation. Ignoring the country's serious racial division the *Free Press* proclaimed, "Canada was saved yesterday—from shame, from national humility, from treachery to her Allies, from treason to the holiest cause for which men have ever fought and died."[87]

Dafoe was not unaware of the critical situation caused by the racial rupture of the country. The day after the election he appealed to a French-Canadian friend to counsel the Quebec Liberals against any action that might increase the gravity of the condition. "I do not think," he concluded somewhat condescendingly, "the situation which is full of peril to Canada, can be changed except upon the initiative of Quebec herself."[88] His friend replied coldly that the crisis was the result of the fact that Dafoe himself, who understood Quebec and knew it was not disloyal, had "made racial appeals to the Anglo-

[84]Dafoe Papers, Dafoe to H. E. M. Chrisolm, Oct. 14, 1917.
[85]*Manitoba Free Press*, Nov. 5, 1917.
[86]*Ibid.*, Dec. 7, 1917.
[87]*Ibid.*, Dec. 18, 1917.
[88]Dafoe Papers, Dafoe to Thomas Coté, Dec. 18, 1917.

Saxon element in the West against the Province of Quebec."[89] The charge was just. In his ardour to ensure the success of the war effort, a cause which Dafoe placed above all others, he had contributed his share to the grim disunity which faced Canadians at Christmas, 1917. But that disunity had not been created *ex nihilo* by conscription. Disunity is always a potential danger in Canada. The ugly sore of racial friction had been irritated by the years of debate over imperial policy and the naval question; the language controversy and the Lapointe resolution brought it to a head only to have it burst explosively by the conscription crisis. At each stage of this ulcerous development Dafoe had played his part. By 1917 he had reached the conclusion that the national interest was so critically at stake that, though racial disharmony might result, a greater cause had to be served, the cause of winning the war. He chose his side and fought for it passionately as an honest, though sometimes unfair, partisan.

As the New Year approached, the Canadian political scene was freer of confusion than it had been for many months. But this confusion had only been erased at the price of a bitter, though peaceful, political revolution. Dafoe, like many thousands of western Canadians, had cut the Gordian knot which for years past had tied him to the Liberal party. Why had this radical step been taken? Laurier offered a cryptic explanation when he wrote of Dafoe, "On many things he has the most advanced ideas of Liberalism and even Radicalism; on others his horizon is the horizon of the sixteenth century."[90] There was certainly truth in Laurier's temperate judgment. Since 1911, Dafoe had been growing increasingly uneasy about the conservatism of the Liberal party, especially on tariff policy. His sympathies were with the western farmer while Laurier, hoping to rebuild a national party, refused to accept the full measure of western demands, knowing that to do so would weaken his position in the more powerful, and more conservative, East.[91] Moreover Dafoe and Laurier disagreed completely on the French-language question. By characterizing him as "sixteenth century" Laurier meant that Dafoe was militantly Protestant in his attitude to the Roman Catholic Church. Certainly Dafoe had a Protestant's suspicion of "clerical influence" and an Anglo-Saxon's belief in the innate superiority of his culture over that of the French Canadians. He believed that with the exception of Quebec, Canada was an English-speaking nation. Therefore his genuine concern to reform the Manitoba school system, and his belief that outside Quebec the French Canadians were without legal language privileges, brought

89*Ibid.*, Thomas Coté to Dafoe, Dec. 27, 1917.
90Laurier Papers, Laurier to A. W. McLeod, Jan. 24, 1918.
91*Ibid.*, Laurier to E. W. Nesbitt, Dec. 23, 1910.

him into conflict with the French-Canadian Liberals. In theory he admitted an historic claim to special treatment for the French Canadians, but in practice he allowed almost none. His suspicions of the French Canadians, aroused by the Lapointe resolution, were further confirmed by Quebec's opposition to conscription and Union government.

But the source of the rupture between Dafoe and Laurier over conscription and Union government was deeper than the Liberal leader was prepared to recognize. It stemmed from a fundamental difference over the nature of the Great War and the role Canada should play in it. From the very outbreak of the conflict Dafoe had taken the view that it was Canada's war and that Canada's interests and aspirations were wagered upon its outcome. Of course, Canada was fighting on the side of Great Britain, but that was not because Canada was a colony, but because the interests of Canada and Great Britain in the cause of "freedom and democracy" were identical. Since it was Canada's war, Dafoe refused to accept any suggestion that limitations be placed on the extent of the country's participation. When voluntary recruiting proved incapable of producing the men necessary for a maximum war effort, Dafoe immediately agreed that compulsory military service would have to be put into practice. Union government was the best available means of achieving this end.

Laurier viewed the war as Britain's war and Canada's contribution to it as the assistance given by a colony to the mother country. This was the central theme of his speech on the declaration of war in the Canadian House of Commons on August 19, 1914: "More than once I have declared that if England were ever in danger—nay, not only in danger, but if she were ever engaged in such a contest as would put her strength to the test—then it would be the duty of Canada to assist the motherland to the utmost of Canada's ability."[92] Again and again the Liberal leader emphasized that Canada was entering the war because Britain was at war and "to ensure the defence of Canada and give what aid may be in our power to the Mother Country."[93] Canadians, he continued, "stood behind the Mother Country, conscious and proud that she was engaged in this war."[94] He made it clear that in his view the defence of Canada was the defence of Canadian territory.[95] Legally, he took the correct position expressed in the maxim, "When Britain is at war, Canada is at war." But since Canada was fighting for Britain, she would not be called upon to make the same sacrifice as the

[92]A. B. Keith, *Select Documents and Speeches on British Colonial Policy, 1763–1917* (Toronto, 1953), 360.
[93]*Ibid.*, 357.
[94]*Ibid.*, 358.
[95]*Ibid.*, 358–9.

principal participants. For Laurier that sacrifice fell just short of conscription. Searching for the cause of his disagreement with Laurier, Dafoe perceptively placed his finger on this crucial point. Characterizing Laurier's viewpoint, Dafoe wrote in his *Sifton*, "The war was England's; Canada was to assist; her assistance, humble as it might be, would be appreciated both for its material value and its moral help."[96] Here Dafoe was giving a telescoped paraphrase of Laurier's peroration. In words that must have stuck in the mind of the Conservative member for Portage la Prairie, Arthur Meighen, and caused Henri Bourassa to shudder, Laurier declared exultantly in August, 1914:

> it is the opinion of the British Government, as disclosed by the correspondence which was brought down to us yesterday, that the assistance of our troops, humble as it may be, will be appreciated, either for its material value, or for the greater moral help which will be rendered. It will be seen by the world, that Canada, a daughter of old England, intends to stand by her in this great conflict. When the call goes out, our answer goes at once, and it goes in the classical language of the British answer to the call to duty: 'Ready, Aye Ready.'[97]

When the conscription issue was raised, Laurier, not for the first time, had more sober thoughts, though his conclusions were implicit in the attitude which he had taken toward the war from the outset. Certainly he had a multiplicity of reasons for opposing conscription—desire to preserve national unity, fear of the reaction in Quebec, doubts about the ability of the measure to produce the promised reinforcements, as well as his pledge to oppose it. But also there was the belief that Canada was engaged in the war not in her own interests, but merely to assist Britain. Describing Laurier's thoughts on conscription, O. D. Skelton wrote revealingly:

> True Britain and the United States had adopted conscription, but they had entered the war as *principals*; it would undermine the whole basis of the Empire, destroy the whole basis of free and friendly *aid and sympathy* if compulsion were resorted to in a country which had gone in, *not for its own sake, but for Britain's.*[98]

Nothing was more indicative of Laurier's attitude than his belief that conscription and Union government were merely aspects of an imperialist plot to centralize the empire according to the plan of the Round Table.[99] Like every other scheme for imperial reorganization, this one had to be resisted.

Laurier's explanation of the reason for Canada's entry into the war was undoubtedly legally correct, and perhaps most Canadians would

[96]Dafoe, *Sifton*, 395.
[97]Keith, *Speeches and Documents*, 362–3.
[98]Skelton, *Laurier*, II, 508–9. My italics.
[99]Laurier Papers, Laurier to Sir Allen Aylesworth, May 15, 1917.

have agreed that Canada was at war to assist Britain. But Dafoe was not one of those Canadians. Regardless of legal technicalities, he believed that Canada was a nation, had entered the war because its interests were at stake, and had to employ every available means to protect them. As he wrote in August, 1917, "Canada is in the war as a principal, not a colony."[100] This had been his position since the day the *Free Press* had announced Canadian involvement in the war.

The nationalism of Dafoe and the nationalism of Laurier were at fundamental variance at this precise point. Dafoe viewed Canada, even in 1914, as part of a wider world in which she had international interests and responsibilities. Laurier saw Canada as isolated from the world and concerned, as far as possible, with her own trying problems. Dafoe's opposition to imperial centralization and the Round Table movement was as tenacious as Laurier's,[101] but whereas Laurier interpreted conscription and Union government as part of a Round Table plot, Dafoe considered them as the necessary means of promoting the national interest. Perhaps this explanation simply describes the gulf between English and French Canadians. But exactly the same conflict arose between Dafoe and Laurier's successor, the English Canadian, Mackenzie King. It arose because Dafoe believed that Canadian nationalism carried obligations as well as status; Laurier and King concentrated their attentions almost exclusively on status. For this reason Dafoe broke with Laurier in 1917, and was severely critical of King's external policy in the inter-war period. Perhaps some benefit might be derived from a fresh consideration of the Laurier-King interpretation of Canadian nationalism. Their interpretation of Canada's position and interest in world affairs is not the only valid one. Dafoe's interpretation was equally valid, and probably more realistic.

[100]*Manitoba Free Press*, Aug. 26, 1917.
[101]Dafoe Papers, Dafoe to G. M. Wrong, Oct. 16, 1916; *Manitoba Free Press*, Aug. 28, 1916. See Donnelly, M. S., "J. W. Dafoe and Lionel Curtis—Two Concepts of the Commonwealth," *Political Studies*, VIII, 2 (June, 1960), 170–82.

The Methodist Church and World War I

J. M. BLISS

THE QUANTITY AND QUALITY of English Canadians' participation in World War I was largely a function of their militant idealism. That idealism was encouraged and sustained by the nation's Christian churches, which, like the churches of every belligerent nation, mobilized all of their spiritual resources for battle. No churchmen in Canada worked harder at hammering their ploughshares into swords than "the people called Methodists." Yet, at the same time as they were preaching a crusade against the German anti-Christ, Methodists in Canada refused to idealize the social order at home. During the war years the Methodist Church's historic concern for social redemption blossomed into a comprehensive programme of social reconstruction. By 1918 the Methodist Church of Canada had become the most radical religious denomination in North America. More clearly than any other group in Canada, the Methodists of 1914–1918 synthesized militarism with a radical social critique.

Few Canadian Methodists worried about war in the spring of 1914. Those who did tended to share the attitude of Dr. W. B. Creighton, editor of the prestigious and widely read *Christian Guardian*, who felt that arms makers were the chief impediments to a peaceful world order. Rather than increase taxes in a militarist cause, Dr. Creighton felt that Canada should withdraw from the arms race and press on Britain her desire for "a broader and more Christian internationalism."[1] Another writer in the *Guardian* called for a general strike by the working class of any nation resorting to war, to be supported by a world boycott of its trade. Under no circumstances was the Christian church to involve itself in support of war of any kind.[2] These pacifist tendencies appeared to have deep roots among Canadian Methodists. As early as 1845 the *Christian Guardian* had condemned both offensive and defensive war

[1]*Christian Guardian*, Jan. 28, April 15, 1914.
[2]*Ibid.*, Jan. 28, 1914.

Reprinted from *Canadian Historical Review*, XLIX (3), September, 1968

as contrary to Christian faith and practice. At every quadrennial conference but one since its formation in 1884 the Methodist Church of
Canada had called for the substitution of arbitration for war. At its 1902
conference, however, the church had condoned the Boer War as being
waged, "not for greed or conquest, but for freedom, for just and honest
government." In fact the church's tradition of pacifist statement has to
be measured against its proclaimed support of every British war after
and including the opium wars.[3] Ripples from the world tide of peace
sentiment increased the volume of pacifist rhetoric in Edwardian Canada. They did not produce a serious re-examination of the ethics of war.

On August 12, 1914, the *Guardian* defined the war as a defensive
struggle against the mediaeval despotism of the Kaiser. The time for
fighting had come. But for the next six weeks or so most churchmen
limited themselves to the fatalism of the writer of Ecclesiastes. Com-
mentators wondered if Britain and France had not been overly jealous
in preventing Russia and Germany from claiming their rightful places
on the world stage and whether Christians who had prayed for peace
while preparing for war could be entirely absolved from responsibility
for the conflict.[4] The earliest atrocity stories were disregarded, as "the
German nation as such is as humane and kindly as our own."[5] Christian
doctrine required loving one's enemies. War was criminal and un-
Christian. We hang murderers, wrote Dr. Creighton, "but in this climax
of national folly we adjudge the prize to him who is the best butcher of
his fellows, and the nation which destroys the most life and property
is hailed as the victor and lauded as one enjoying the special favour of
the gods."[6] God must not be asked for victory: "All that we can do is
pray 'God pity us all, God forgive us all, God show us a better and a
holier and a more brotherly way of life.' "[7] The church was going to war,
but with a twofold purpose according to the Rev. Ernest Thomas: "on
the one hand to support with hallowed fire the glow of loyalty and
devotion, and at the same time with a strong hand purge that loyalty
of its blatant and sordid features."[8]

In the autumn of 1914, however, church leaders abandoned their
critical acquiescence in war in favour of an unquestioning belief in the
righteousness of the conflict and the church's duty to play a positive
role in achieving victory. Samuel Dwight Chown, the church's general
superintendent, had wired Ottawa on August 5 offering his services in

[3]M. V. Royce, *The Contribution of the Methodist Church to Social Welfare in Canada*,
unpublished M.A. thesis, University of Toronto, 1938, pp. 268–78.
[4]*Christian Guardian*, Aug. 12, Sept. 16, 1914.
[5]*Ibid.*, Sept. 30, 1914.
[6]*Ibid.*, Aug. 19, 1914.
[7]*Ibid.*, Aug. 12, 1914.
[8]*Ibid.*, Sept. 16, 1914. Thomas wrote under the pen name of "Edward Trelawney."

any capacity. Since then he had been tramping the hills of British Columbia conditioning himself for possible service as a combatant—at age sixty-one.[9] In the middle of September he published his first open letter to Methodists on the war; it set out the view of the war from which the church would never again vary:

We are persuaded that this war is just, honorable and necessary in defence of the principle of righteousness and the freedom of our Empire in all its parts. We believe it to be a world struggle for liberty against military despotism which, if successful, would make our life not worth living. . . . We are constrained to applaud, and with all our power endorse, the drawing of the sword by Great Britain and Canada. . . . To our people, loyal Methodists and true, I would say—enlist in the Canadian army, unless you feel you can serve the Dominion better at home in peaceful avocations than in the thickest of the fight. When that conviction gives way, go to the front bravely as one who hears the call of God.[10]

All of the allied nations were absolved from blame as Methodist writers, assisted by government-sponsored pamphlets, uncovered Germany's responsibility for the outbreak of war and explained the militarism inherent in German civilization. The Old Testament provided a useful interpretive framework: the German Sennacherib had descended out of the night on Hezekiah (Belgium); alternatively, Germany's envy of Britain and France led to war as surely as Haman's jealousy for Mordecai the Israelite led him to try to slay the Hebrews. It was comforting to realize that Haman had been hanged and that the people of Sennacherib had been smitten "an hundred four-score and five thousand" by the angel of the Lord.[11] By the summer of 1915 the wave of atrocity stories had convinced Methodists that the Germans did not fight like other nations. Like most Canadians, Methodists eventually believed they were fighting a people that inoculated its captives with tuberculosis, decorated its dwellings with human skin, crucified Canadian soldiers, and enforced a national policy of compulsory polygamy on its virgins.[12] Analysts who had at first argued that a basically Christian people had been misled by the Kaiser's worship of Woden now decided that Christianity had been extinguished among the whole German people so that German religion had become the exact antithesis of Christianity.[13] Methodist leaders nevertheless insisted on some form of humanitarian concern for the German people until well into 1917.[14]

Despite the accumulated evidence that this was a war worth fighting

[9]United Church Archives (UCA), S. D. Chown Papers, undated "Address on the Abolition of War."
[10]*Christian Guardian*, Sept. 16, 1914.
[11]*Ibid.*, Nov. 18, 1914; Jan. 13, 1915.
[12]*Ibid.*, Oct. 10, 1917; Sept. 11, Oct. 23, 1918.
[13]*Ibid.*, Feb. 10, 1915; Nov. 1, 1916.
[14]By 1918 Methodists were ready to hang the Kaiser and make Germany pay the total costs of the war. At no time had they supported any of the peace proposals.

for, Christians were faced with the special problem of reconciling their support for war with those statements of Jesus which seemed to deny the use of violence in any circumstances. For the first three years of the war a handful of pacifist critics periodically challenged the editor of the *Guardian* to explain his trust in bullets rather than bibles or to imagine St. John plunging his bayonet through the heart of a fellow man. A pacifist contributed one of the better poems published in the *Guardian* in 1915:

> I heard the rumble of distant guns,
> And I saw mad, marching men.
> Each man was flinging his life away
> For a God he'd found again;
> An old God laughing at war and might,
> But Christ I saw not marching that night.[15]

Dr. Creighton responded by arguing that Christians must use force to defend the right until all men renounce violence.[16] His arguments were reasonably sophisticated; more commonly, pacifists were challenged with images of ruffians attacking their wives and children. Most Methodists agreed with Dr. Chown's view of Christ's probable behaviour:

For myself it is enough to know that Christ, as I perceive Him, would not stand with limp hands if a ruthless soldier should attempt to outrage His holy mother as the women of Belgium were violated. To Him all motherhood is sacred; nor would He retreat and give place to the armed burglar, breaking with murderous intent into His home; nor would He witness, without any effort to prevent it, the destruction of the civil and religious liberty which His teaching has enthroned in our British Empire. His manhood is without seam throughout, and I believe Canada is right in this war.[17]

There is no evidence to suggest that any significant body of Methodists openly opposed the war. The only notable Methodist ministers who appear to have been pacifists were J. S. Woodsworth and William Ivens in Winnipeg. Neither spoke out more than a handful of times against the war. Western Canada's most popular Methodist, Salem Bland, staunchly supported Canada's efforts in both world wars. (An error in the *Canadian Annual Review* for 1915 has misled some writers into seeing Bland as a pacifist.) In attempting to win the Unionist nomination for Winnipeg Centre in the 1917 election Bland was "first and foremost . . . heart and soul for the war."[18] On at least one occasion he spoke of it as the noblest, divinest cause the world had ever known.[19]

The war did become a divine cause for Canadian Methodists. By the end of the first year of war the church had "transfigured" the war into a

---

[15]*Christian Guardian*, May 5, 1915.
[16]*Ibid.*, Jan. 27, Oct. 6, 1915.
[17]*Ibid.*, Aug. 23, 1916.
[18]UCA, Salem Bland Papers, "Nomination Address," Aug. 14, 1917.
[19]*Ibid.*, undated clipping included in sermon "Cheering Thoughts on a Dark Day."

crusade for Christianity rather than a simple defence of liberty. Both Dr. Chown and Dr. Creighton came to identify Germany with the anti-Christ, the struggle as a clash between eternal principles of good and evil, and allied soldiers as the instruments of God. In November 1915 Wesley College (Winnipeg) told its students at the front: "It is God's battle you are fighting in Flanders and at the Dardanelles, as English-men fought it when they scattered the Armada in wild flight, as Israel fought it when they overthrew Philistine or Midianite. . . . By a sad necessity, the highest service to the kingdom of God on earth has become the service to which you have consecrated your manhood."[20] By 1918 the dominant Methodist attitude to the war was a simple belief in the literal truth of the words of the church's favourite wartime hymn: "The Son of God goes forth to war, / A kingly crown to gain; / His blood red banner streams afar; / Who follows in his train?"

The most immediate consequence of the church's crusading posture was its support of recruiting. Ministers and students enlisted to a total of almost five hundred by the end of the war. Roughly 90 per cent of the Methodist clergy who served were combatants.[21] This remarkably high figure illustrates the intensity of Methodist support and verifies the assumption that the clergy saw themselves as fighting a holy war. Pacifists who objected to preachers carrying rifles were reminded that Christians must practise what they preach.

By spring of 1915 the tide of patriotic fervour among Canadian men had begun to ebb ever so slightly. The churches began to play an active role in recruiting. In March Dr. Chown began asking every young man at patriotic meetings to give an account of himself "to his Empire and to God why he is not in khaki" which was now "a sacred color."[22] In June the *Guardian* began to carry articles on the duty of Methodists to serve their country; by August it was able to note that pulpits had been the best recruiting stations in the first year of the war.[23] A number of ministers noted for their patriotic addresses were appointed recruiting directors early in 1916. Four of the seven clergymen involved were Methodists, including the Rev. C. A. Williams of St. James Church, Montreal, who won a special place in history as the English Protestant in charge of Quebec's recruiting.[24] In December 1915 the church's Army and Navy Board asked each minister to supply the names of the men in his community "who should respond to the call," promising that "this valuable information would be properly used without revealing

[20]*Christian Guardian*, Nov. 10, 1915.
[21]*Journal of Proceedings of the Tenth General Conference of the Methodist Church* (Toronto, 1918), pp. 140–1.
[22]*Christian Guardian*, March 15, 1915.
[23]*Ibid.*, Aug. 4, 1915.
[24]*Canadian Annual Review*, 1916, p. 305.

your name."[25] The recruiting drive reached a crescendo in the autumn of 1916 when the *Guardian* itself was turned into a clearing house for recruits and a great Methodist patriotic meeting in Toronto was the signal for similar meetings in every district of the church in Canada.[26]

The church's Army and Navy Board organized all of these meetings. It suggested that the chairman of each district have a small advertisement placed in local newspapers on the day of each meeting, "not so much to get an audience as to insure the attendance of reporters and get a good report in the press."[27] Good reports in the press had become important in 1916 because of widespread complaints that Methodists were letting down their nation in its time of crisis. Anglicans were doing most of the complaining, having discovered that their denomination was supplying more than half of the recruits for the Canadian army. (The government had conveniently released figures on recruitment according to religious denomination.) Anglican mathematicians calculated that the Methodist Church was sending only 50 per cent of its "share" of recruits, the lowest percentage of any Protestant denomination.[28] Anglicans worried aloud about "the stain of failure in national duty" of Methodism.[29] The Methodist hierarchy responded with complaints that the government's religious categories were inaccurate and biased. Dr. Chown vowed in 1918 that Methodists "do not now and never will accept" the government's figures.[30] But two years previously the Army and Navy Board had told the Methodist clergy in a confidential letter that its own tabulations substantially agreed with the government's totals. The figures showed, the board complained, "that in this awful crisis in British history and Christian civilization the Methodist Church is not playing a noble part."[31]

Reluctant young men faced almost irresistible pressures to enlist. When direct appeals to patriotic and Christian loyalties were ignored, the church urged its women to encourage their husbands and sons to protect them from "the outrage which overtook Belgian women at the beginning of the war."[32] In their section of the *Guardian* children were taught to badger young men on the street in the hope of shaming them

[25]UCA, Methodist Church Army and Navy Board, Correspondence, General Letter, Dec. 22, 1915.

[26]UCA, Army and Navy Board, *Minutes*, Nov. 13, 1916. J. S. Woodsworth's description of a typical Methodist patriotic service is quoted in Kenneth McNaught, *A Prophet in Politics* (Toronto, 1959), p. 70.

[27]Army and Navy Board, *Minutes*, Nov. 13, 1916.

[28]Toronto *Mail and Empire*, Sept. 19, 1916, letter to the editor.

[29]*Canadian Churchman*, Oct. 5, 1916.

[30]*Journal of Proceedings, Tenth General Conference*, p. 143.

[31]Army and Navy Board, Correspondence, undated letter, "The Methodist Church and the British Flag."

[32]Chown Papers, "War Address," Aug. 4, 1915.

into enlisting.[33] Narrowly selfish mothers were condemned for bringing up sons with no sense of duty or responsibility: "Such mothers train degenerate sons."[34] In November 1916 an eligible young man wrote to the *Guardian* explaining the impossibility of his enlisting without completely ruining the thriving business he had built up from nothing in his community. After two years of war, "I cannot go to a public meeting, I cannot walk down the street, I cannot go to Sunday School, League or Church, I cannot attend any of the District conventions, I cannot even go home and read *Youth and Service* or *The Guardian* without being told I am a shirker."[35] Should he enlist or quit the church and all public meetings until after the war? He was advised to enlist.

Every other facet of the domestic war effort was fully supported by the church. Methodist women joined in the sewing and knitting campaigns which must have made Canadian soldiers the best clothed, best bandaged fighting men in the history of warfare. Boston baked beans became the main course at church suppers; at home Methodist families trimmed their menus to the bone. Their children sublimated their taste for sweets to save their pennies for Belgian relief. Ministers made church land free for cultivation, preached sermons on methods of increasing food production, and went into the fields themselves to help with 1917's harvest. Methodist churches opened their recreation rooms to returned soldiers and men on leave. St. James Church in Montreal allowed smoking and billiards in its basement despite its secretary's fears that St. James might go the way of the Parliament Buildings and a billiard company's complaints that its minister was unfit to be a recruiting officer because his church did business with a German billiard table firm.[36] Presumably Methodists contributed heavily to the Victory Loan after Dr. Chown defined it as a proposition on which "we shall save or lose our souls."[37]

The most important aspect of the church's war effort was intangible. Any secular institution could organize recruiting drives, knitting bees, or conservation campaigns. Only the churches had the ideological resources to provide solace and comfort to the discouraged, the frightened, the despairing, and the mourning. There is no way of determining the contribution to national morale made by the zealous and sincere minister planning his Sunday evening patriotic service, organizing a midweek prayer meeting, or finding time to pay a special visit to the family whose son had been reported missing in action. Because the

[33]*Christian Guardian*, Dec. 13, 1916.
[34]*Ibid.*, Nov. 1, 1916.
[35]*Ibid.*, Nov. 15, 1916.
[36]UCA, Methodist Church, Correspondence, J. H. Carson to S. D. Chown, Feb. 25, 1916; *Beck's Weekly Tattler*, April 1, 1916.
[37]Toronto *Globe*, Nov. 26, 1917.

Canadian community was profoundly Christian before and during World War I, it is highly questionable whether its citizens could have endured the emotional nightmare of war without the sustaining belief that God was on their side, that their loved ones were only doing their duty to God and their country, and that death, if it came, was only *The Beautiful Thing That Has Happened to Our Boys.*[38] Those families who doubted that their sons had walked the straight path before they went off to fight were assured that soldiers learned to pray in the trenches. Even mothers with openly irreligious sons could rest at ease, "... because this war, unless we are the victims of some terrible delusion, and all our thinking and teaching, praying and preaching, is utterly false, is God's war, and doing our bit in any capacity to help win it is a supreme manifestation of faith, a supreme act of decision and of sacrifice for Christ."[39]

The crises of 1917 show how completely Methodists identified the war effort with practical Christianity. In the autumn of 1916 Methodist leaders began to call for conscription. When a scheme of national service was initiated at the beginning of 1917, Dr. Chown officially urged ministers "to stimulate conformity to the desire of the Government in this hour of national peril" on the scriptural ground that shirkers were clearly immoral: " 'If *any* man will not work, neither shall he eat.' "[40] In June every Methodist conference resolved in favour of conscription; most also called for a union government.[41] The Union government and its policy of conscription were duly approved of by Methodist leaders. In the December election Methodists, like most other Protestant churchmen, threw open their pulpits to Unionist speakers and their church halls to Unionist election meetings. Resolutions were passed on all levels of the church organization favouring the Unionist cause. The *Guardian* actively supported the Unionists. Dr. Chown issued a lengthy open letter explaining why he favoured the government; excerpts from it were published in leading newspapers by the Unionist party publicity committee. Disclaiming any intention of dictating to Methodists how they should vote, the executive of the Board of Social Service and Evangel-

---

[38]By Charles Allen; available for fifty cents from the church publishing house. *Christian Guardian*, Jan. 7, 1917, advertisement.

[39]*Christian Guardian*, June 6, 1917.

[40]*Ibid.*, Jan. 3, 1917.

[41]It is not clear how representative of local sentiment these resolutions were. T. Albert Moore, secretary of the Army and Navy Board, had visited each conference specifically to plead for conscription and union government. He described the results of his work in a long letter to the Prime Minister, who replied that "the approval of the various conferences of the Methodist Church must have a notable effect in influencing public opinion along the right lines with respect to Compulsory Military Service." Army and Navy Board, Correspondence, T. A. Moore to R. L. Borden, June 14, 1917; Borden to Moore, June 25, 1917.

ism issued a statement to be read in every pulpit explaining its support of the Union government and urging: "At the polls on December 17th, 1917, every Methodist elector, the women as well as the men, should conscientiously meet personal responsibility and both vote and work for the election of candidates which [sic] stand with the Union Government."[42] In a day when few ministers openly engaged in politics Dr. Salem Bland attempted to win the Unionist nomination for Winnipeg Centre. He was rejected because of his political unorthodoxy; one writer called him "a sort of Independent-Labor-Socialist-Free-Trade-and-What-Not-Candidate."[43] Nevertheless, he continued to support the Unionist cause.

Methodists accepted the Unionist claim that a Liberal victory would mean Canada's withdrawal from the war. The election became a plebiscite on the righteousness of the crusade. Dr. Chown interpreted political duty in exclusively religious categories:

This is a redemptive war, and its success depends entirely on the height of sacrifice to which our people can ascend. It is under this conviction that ministers of the gospel feel in duty bound to enter the political arena. We shall fail and fail lamentably as Christians unless we catch the martyr spirit of true Christianity and do our sacrificial duty between now and on the 17th of December. But if we fail, I, for one, will never be sorry that I tried to bear aloft the banner of the cross amidst the tumult of the fight.[44]

Earlier in the war the church had spoken out strongly against a wartime election on the ground that partisanship would confuse and divide the national purpose. Now there was only one party attempting to divide the national will, and its patriotic wing had rejected partisanship. This showed that the election was no ordinary political struggle. Dr. Chown wrote of the conscriptionist Liberals: "To permit such patriots to be defeated would be to doom all independence of political thought and action in Canada, and forge the shackles of blind partisanship upon us, with its accompaniment of corrupt patronage and all that such a system entails, for generations to come. Now is the time for Canada to strike for freedom from the system of political grafting."[45] Methodists had traditionally blamed the patronage that flowed from partisanship for most of the evils in Canadian political life. They had condemned the Borden government for its corruption; but now it had disappeared into the coalition. Even in peacetime Methodists would have been delighted with a movement that promised to cure the political ills of the nation.

Racial and religious antipathies were kept more or less under control

[42]*Globe*, Dec. 8, 1917; *Christian Guardian*, Dec. 12, 1917.
[43]Bland Papers, clipping in "Union Government" portfolio.
[44]*Christian Guardian*, Dec. 12, 1917.
[45]*Ibid.*

48 J. M. BLISS

in the *Guardian*. Condemnations of Quebec's recruiting record were
usually well qualified. In the election campaign Dr. Creighton cautioned
against racial bitterness: ". . . we are persuaded that the great mass of
the Quebec people are loyal to the Empire and sanely law-abiding, and
the wild utterances of a few political firebrands are not to be taken as
reflecting the feelings or sentiments of the people of the province as a
whole."[46] Dr. Chown was less moderate. He had privately written in
1916: "Is it fair to leave the Province of Quebec to retain its strength
in numbers, ready for any political or military aggression in the future,
while our Protestants go forth to slaughter and decimation?"[47] He
warned publicly in 1917 that a Liberal victory would give "one type of
religion . . . a prepondering influence in the counsels of the Government
of Canada."[48] Probably Dr. Chown's sentiments approximate Methodist
opinion at the circuit level.

The Military Voters' Act and the War-time Elections Act were also
approved by the church. Dr. Creighton had come to believe that German behaviour in Europe made it impossible to trust any German:
"There can be no apology for . . . [disfranchisement] except the fact that
just now there are few, if any, Canadians who believe that these Ger-
man-born Canadian citizens desire that Britain should win the war. . . .
The Anglo-Saxon is not usually suspicious, but he has learned at last to
suspect the German."[49] Scattered through the church records are complaints about pro-German American periodicals, reports of invitations
to American speakers with neutralist tendencies being withdrawn, and
letters suggesting that there was no place in Canadian Methodism for
the opinions of pacifists. After conscription was enacted Methodist
ministers played a leading part in alerting the Saskatchewan government to the "Mennonite menace" and suggested that the policy of
exempting Mennonites be reviewed.[50] In Guelph, Ontario, the Rev.
H. G. Christie led the city's Protestant ministers into battle against the
nearby Jesuit novitiate college by charging that some of the college's
recently accepted novitiates, including the Hon. C. J. Doherty's son,
were draft dodgers. This incensed one Ontario MLA into charging that
"the greatest menace to the Province of Ontario is the Methodist
Church . . . ."[51] The Methodist Church was certainly a menace to the
conscientious objector. Accepting the biblical injunction, "If any man
will not work, neither shall he eat," the *Guardian* was willing to support
measures to make conscientious objectors literal "outlaws":

[46]*Ibid.*, Nov. 14, 1917.
[47]Army and Navy Board, Correspondence, S. D. Chown to K. Kingston, Nov. 30, 1916.
[48]*Christian Guardian*, Dec. 12, 1917.
[49]*Ibid.*, Sept. 26, 1917.
[50]*Ibid.*, Oct. 9, 1918.
[51]*Canadian Annual Review*, 1918, pp. 457–61.

We may not feel like forcing such a man to fight, nor like punishing him for his honest opinions; but if he be honest, then let him be prepared to take the full consequences of his opinions. If he does not believe it is right to fight in defence of his privileges as a citizen, then let him refuse to allow those privileges to be maintained by the efforts of others. . . . According to this theory such a man would have no legal rights. He could not vote, he could not hold property, he could not in case of any invasion of his rights call upon the Government or the courts for protection.[52]

In 1918 Methodists decided that pacifism was no longer a legitimate Christian doctrine. The *Guardian* had repeatedly warned against the evil consequences of "knocking" the war effort. Critics of the war were too often the people who had never done anything for the empire; with any sense they would use their right of free speech with discretion. Until 1918, however, the *Guardian's* correspondence columns were open to dissenters. In March of that year Dr. Creighton concluded that pacifism could not be tolerated "no matter who may teach it."[53] A frontispiece in April was entitled "The Vice of Pacifism"; it commended to Methodists Moses' action in killing the Egyptian slave driver he found beating an Israelite.[54] On May 1, probably in part because of the recent Order-in-Council suppressing seditious and antiwar opinions, the *Guardian* silenced the pacifists within the Church:

In time of war any type of religion which is pro-German is not a desirable type for this country, and any type which is not ardently pro-British and pro-American is not very much better. The matter of conscience does not change these facts, and a conscience which does not sanction patriotism is a very poor affair. . . .
. . . where the man's conscience is of such a stubborn type that it refuses to admit that a victory for the Allies is any more to be desired than a victory for the Germans . . . no plea of Christian liberty and of freedom of speech can be allowed for a moment, any more than we would allow it in a case where a man preached free love or polygamy. It is not a case of conscience, but a case of Christian morals, and the sin of unpatriotic speech and act is one which the Church cannot afford to condone.

J. S. Woodsworth had been drifting away from orthodoxy for a number of years. His church's attitude towards the war, particularly its expression in this editorial, drove him to insist that his resignation from the ministry be accepted.[55] It is essential to note that Woodsworth was the only major figure in Methodism to leave the church because of the war. The most significant protests against the church's leadership were made on the issue of political control during the 1917 election. At that time a few congregations were disrupted, members of one congregation

[52]*Christian Guardian*, Aug. 8, 1917.
[53]*Ibid.*, March 6, 1918.
[54]*Ibid.*, April 3, 1918.
[55]McNaught, *A Prophet in Politics*, pp. 82–7.

came to blows during Sunday worship, several ministers were intimidated into keeping silent, and a several months' controversy raged in the correspondence columns of the *Guardian*.[56] But feelings were assuaged without any recorded ministerial resignations or seceding congregations. The wartime dismissals of Salem Bland and William Ivens from appointments in Winnipeg were not related to their attitudes on the war.

The Methodist Church's social conscience was in no way stifled by its patriotism. How could a denomination as outspoken in its denunciation of national sinfulness as Methodism had been proclaim honestly that the existence of a truly Christian civilization was now at stake? Methodists insisted that in a war of ideals the right ideals must prevail at home. A righteous war would have to end with Canada nearer the kingdom of righteousness. Many Methodists thought the war would not end until Canada did come closer to that kingdom. Underlying prayers for victory and assurances that the outcome of the war was in God's hands was a strong current of feeling that somehow God was punishing Canadians for their sins. Dr. Chown asked Methodists to pray that God would "show us wherein our sins have unfitted us to be the servants of Jehovah in bringing the reign of peace to the heart of this troubled world."[57] The Rev. Nathanael Burwash, formerly a leader in the fight for a liberal interpretation of Scripture, meditated on the sins of the Israelites and concluded: "It would seem as if we had repeated all the national and personal sins of this ancient people. And now we, like them, are passing under God's rod. . . . Just now in God's presence we should remember only that *we have sinned*. Our penitent prayers will bring the answer of peace when we open the way to God's forgiveness by turning away from the sins which have called for this terrible chastising."[58] For perhaps the wrong reasons Methodists rightly concluded that the allied nations shared the responsibility for the war. They were determined that it would never happen again.

The records of the church's 1914 quadrennial conference show a dualistic concern with complex social problems on the one hand and the traditional varieties of individual sin on the other hand. A carefully phrased "statement regarding Sociological questions" is matched by a nine-page report on the temperance movement. While its Committee of Social Service and Evangelism called for the abolition of poverty, a minimum wage, and an equitable partnership between employer and employee, the Department of Temperance, Prohibition, and Moral Reform concentrated on its attempts to redeem "lost women," its quest to

[56]*Globe*, Dec. 17, 1917; *Christian Guardian*, January and February 1918.
[57]*Christian Guardian*, Dec. 22, 1915.
[58]*Ibid.*, March 20, 1918.

discover and restore victims of the white slaver, and the problems of the seduction of female employees and the age of consent. The conclusion of the department's report reflects the secondary importance of the social gospel in Methodist thought: "Christ's witnesses must survey, chart, invade, and conquer the world for Him. The drunkenness, the vice, the violence, the industrial injustice, the indecent theatres, the immoral cafes, cabarets and hotels, the moral slaughter of girlhood and youth connected with the evil business of the Twentieth century, call out the old challenge to Christ's people, 'Watchman, what of the night?' "[59]

The war was a godsend to the temperance movement. Who could deny the proposition that "the beer-befuddled soldier is a poor defence to his country?"[60] The liquor interests became "the worst pro-Germans we have in Canada to-day, the most treasonable persons."[61] Well into 1915 Methodists insisted that "King alcohol" was a greater menace to Canadians than all the Kaiser's legions. Playing on the nation's concern for its soldiers and food supplies, as well as the desire to make tangible sacrifices, the temperance forces had won their battle by 1917 in every province but Quebec. Seven days after the 1917 election the Union government announced that the importation of liquor would be prohibited. Unionist leaders were probably not surprised to read of Methodist ministers announcing that their vote for the Union government was already justified.[62]

But on Salisbury Plain in 1914 General Alderson had told the men of the first contingent of the CEF that they were men and proceeded to open a wet canteen. Speaking for Canadian Methodists, Dr. Chown questioned General Alderson's "moral right" to thus treat Canadian motherhood.[63] For the next four years petitions against the wet canteen and the fraud involved in shipping the rum ration to the front disguised as medical supplies regularly descended on Ottawa. The largest petition was signed by 64,000 mothers and wives of Ontario. All petitions were forwarded to the British government.

Many Canadian Methodists came to believe that sex and liquor in England were worse threats to Canadian manhood than the guns in France. Methodist ministers protested against the government's interpretation of "bad" books when it proscribed pamphlets put out by British temperance organizations.[64] After exhaustive investigations in

[59]*Journal of Proceedings of the Ninth General Conference of the Methodist Church* (Toronto, 1914), p. 266.
[60]*Christian Guardian*, Nov. 18, 1914.
[61]*Ibid.*, Sept. 22, 1915.
[62]*Globe*, Dec. 24, 1917.
[63]*Canadian Annual Review*, 1914, p. 206.
[64]For correspondence on the topic see Public Archives of Canada, R. L. Borden Papers,

Great Britain in 1917 Dr. Chown stated on his return to Canada that
the boys "were submitted to greater temptations in London than they
should be called upon to bear."[65] In his private report to the Army and
Navy Board, however, he admitted that drunkenness and venereal
disease were not major problems among Canadian soldiers. (Most of
the venereal disease, he felt, was confined to the British-born majority
of the CEF. British officials countered by claiming that most of the
stricken had been infected in Canada.[66])

The church's concern for the moral health of Canadian soldiers
probably hurt its own recruiting efforts. Fear of the consequences for
recruiting must have been the reason for the censorship of British temperance pamphlets. Castell Hopkins concluded that Canadian moral
asceticism had hindered recruiting: "The extreme degree to which
objection to liquor and the smoking of cigarettes had been bred made
domestic sentiment against the Army—smoking in the trenches or a
wet canteen at the Front—very vigorous; . . ."[67] Dr. Chown was so
distressed by the liquor trade in England that he held private doubts
whether the English nation was worth fighting for.[68]

The war years marked the apogee of moral fundamentalism in Canada. Neither the nation as a whole, fed up with sacrifice, nor its returned
fighting men, impatient with what seemed to be the trivia of a provincial
society, would ever again approach the wartime pitch of hatred for
"King alcohol" and its concomitant vices. By 1922 only 35,000 Methodist Sunday school members had signed pledge cards; in 1916 the total
had been 118,000.[69] Movements to interdict the spread of smoking were
drowned by protests that tobacco was essential to the mental health of
the fighting men. Sabbatarianism suffered from the necessity for full
use of productive facilities. The first chinks in Methodism's wall of

---

OC 387. One of the prohibited pamphlets, Arthur Mee's *The Fiddlers*, describes hundreds
of incidents similar to the following:
"A boy got his V.C., and came home wounded. The publican in his street sounded
his praises in the taproom, where they subscribed to the bar for 120 pints for him when
he arrived. He came home and began to drink it, and was nearly dead with it before
he was rescued." (p. 23)
"A Canadian soldier, helplessly drunk, was seen at King's Cross Station tearing,
crumpling up, and eating one pound notes, and would have lost about fifteen pounds
but for kindly help from passers-by." (p. 37)
"A Sergeant-Major from Canada declared that he had lost 20 per cent. of the men
of his battery through venereal disease. They had a little drink, and were captured by
the swarm of bad women at Folkestone." (p. 38)
[65]*Christian Guardian*, Sept. 26, 1917.
[66]Army and Navy Board, Correspondence, undated report, S. D. Chown to the board.
[67]*Canadian Annual Review*, 1915, p. 217.
[68]Army and Navy Board, Correspondence, undated report, S. D. Chown to the board.
[69]*Journal of Proceedings of the Eleventh General Conference of the Methodist Church*
(Toronto, 1922), p. 440; *Journal of Proceedings, Tenth Conference*, p. 434.

ignorance and inhibition about sex were made by the new consciousness of venereal disease ("social disease" before the war) that the war forced on Canadians. Clear-minded Methodists realized what was happening. Dr. Creighton in the *Guardian* admitted that under the stress of war "the great majority of us feel that to some degree at least old restrictions and habits must yield."[70]

Relaxed restrictions did not imply a relaxed concern for the health of society. On the contrary, the Methodist social conscience became increasingly sophisticated as churchmen interpreted and applied "The New Things We Are Seeing" on the home front. Within a few months of the outbreak of war Methodists were remarking on the changes that had come over Canada. Dr. Chown felt humanity had been raised up to "one of the highest mountain peaks in the experience of our race," for:

... the Christian ideal of service is displacing all other conceptions of success. The trappings of earthly estates are relegated to oblivion, and only the core of consecrated manhood is held in high esteem in these crucial days. The teachings of Jesus concerning sympathy and self-denial are being accepted by the secular arm as the dominant motives of diplomacy and the very soul of patriotic action.[71]

Dr. Creighton argued that "the fierce furnace of war" was burning up "the waste and rubbish and evil of our lives." Class distinctions, empty pleasure-seeking, indolent shirking of responsibilities were all being replaced by "an instinct of brotherhood and high and holy and self-sacrificing ideas and purposes of life."[72] In the west Salem Bland pictured the war as the beginning of "a new era of redemption" which would feature more government ownership and control, a readjustment in the relations of capital and labour, steps towards the equalization of wealth, the abolition of the competitive principle in Canadian life, and the extension of economic democracy throughout the world.[73]

Methodists expected that all members of a community dedicated to a common goal would sacrifice equally and to the limit. From the moment that war broke out Methodists insisted that profiteering be abolished. That Methodism's leading layman, Joseph Flavelle, was intimately involved in the most sensational of the profiteering inquiries did not deter the *Guardian* from condemning his company's excessive profits.[74] To defend itself the company was forced to take three-page advertisements in the journal. The efforts at food control of W. J. Hanna, a Methodist himself, paled in comparison with Jesus' demonstration of

[70]*Christian Guardian*, April 18, 1917.
[71]*Ibid.*, Oct. 27, 1915.
[72]*Ibid.*, Feb. 9, 1916.
[73]Bland Papers, collection of sermons on the war.
[74]*Christian Guardian*, Nov. 28, July 25, 1917.

what could be done with two loaves and five fishes.[75] Conscription of
wealth was always a part of the Methodist "platform" in 1917. It is not
always realized that the Union government specifically promised to
conscript wealth by taxing war profits and increasing the income tax.[76]
Dr. Creighton ably summed up the church's wartime attitude to business:

The war has taught us many things, and it is teaching us that the right conduct of
business is, after all, fundamentally a national affair, and while individualism must
necessarily prevail to a certain extent, that extent is definitely limited to the point
where it conserves the national wellbeing. Business exists to serve, and not to prey
upon, the life of the community. And whenever business becomes predatory it is
essential to the national wellbeing that it be brought under proper control. The
state has the right to control all business and to wipe out of existence any business
which is a damage to the state. It seems to us that in reaching this point in our
national thinking we have made a distinct and moral advance.[77]

By 1917 Methodist leaders were calling for the application of war
principles in peacetime. If the nation could maintain such unity and
nobility of purpose in war, it could and should continue to do so in
the peacetime struggle against sin. If individual prerogatives such as
the right of private property could be justly sacrificed in the national
interest in wartime, the same sacrifices could be validly called for by
the nation after the war. In the last two years of the war these themes
were outlined a number of times in the *Guardian* by Ernest Thomas,
F. N. Stapleford, and Dr. Creighton. The editor's summary is representative:

The war has been a great leveller, and there is no question that it is causing men
to see, as they never saw before, that manhood is a nation's chief asset, and the old
theory of the sacredness of property is bound to be roughly shouldered aside by
the new theory of the sacredness of life; and in the coming years it seems assured
that this new theory will work mighty changes in our social fabric, and it seems
probable that every one of these changes will be in the direction of righteousness
and justice. A square deal for every man will be the national motto. In this way the
war promises to bring the Kingdom of God nearer to us.[78]

[75]*Ibid.*, May 15, 1918.
[76]Borden Papers, OC 367, *Manifesto of Sir Robert Borden to the Canadian People*,
Nov. 17, 1917.
[77]*Christian Guardian*, April 12, 1916; see also issues of Oct. 11, Nov. 29, 1916. In the
Guardian of Nov. 7, 1917, the Rev. Ernest Thomas called for state controls more rigid
than any existing form of war socialism: "Let the nation lay down for every citizen the
principle that during the war no private person shall be allowed more than is needed to
meet the demands involved in the maintenance of his private business, the demands of
efficient life, and the provision against dependency. Let luxuries be refused any recognition. Let all motor cars used for private pleasure, and all other expenditures on matters
which do not make for social and national efficiency, be prohibited. All the surplus
should go to the nation, which will either assign its citizens a place in the national service
or confirm him [sic] in his present life as one furthering the interests of the nation.
There he may demand the means of efficient living. Beyond that the nation should
tolerate nothing being diverted to private ends."
[78]*Ibid.*, Aug. 29, 1917.

The church's opinion of the new ideas that had captured the *Guardian* was expressed at the 1918 quadrennial conference. The Committee on the Church, the War, and Patriotism presented a report outlining what it understood to be the lessons for Canada and for Methodism of the war. After reminding the delegates that Methodism "was born in a revolt against sin and social extravagance and corruption," the committee pointed out that:

Under the shock and strain of this tremendous struggle, accepted commercial and industrial methods based on individualism and competition have gone down like mud walls in a flood. National organization, national control, extraordinary approximations of national equality have been found essential to efficiency.

Despite the derangements and sorrows of the war, the Motherland has raised large masses of her people from the edge of starvation to a higher plain of physical well-being, and in consequence, was never so healthy, never so brotherly, nor ever actuated by so high a purpose, or possessed by such exaltation of spirit as to-day—and the secret is that all are fighting or working, and all are sacrificing.

It is not inconceivable that when Germany ceases to be a menace, these dearly bought discoveries will be forgotten. Relapse would mean recurrence, the renewal of agony.

The conclusion seems irresistible. The war is a sterner teacher than Jesus and uses far other methods, but it teaches the same lesson. The social development which it has so unexpectedly accelerated has the same goal as Christianity, that common goal is a nation of comrade workers, as now at the trenches, fights so gloriously—a nation of comrade fighters.

Because of these lessons, because the twentieth century had shown that political democracy meant little without economic democracy, and because of the ethics of Jesus, the committee advocated "nothing less than a transference of the whole economic life from a basis of competition and profits to one of co-operation and service." A new system of production and service for human needs rather than for private profit would require the national government to "enlist in the service of the nation" the industrial resources of the country. Joint boards of employers and workers to regulate working conditions on the model of the British Whitley Councils would be one possibility, but only temporarily: ". . . we do not believe this separation of labor and capital can be permanent. Its transcendence, whether through co-operation or public ownership, seems to be the only constructive and radical reform."

Although it had prefaced its argument with a denial that its report bound the church to any specific economic policy, the committee spelled out what acceptance of its report implied: "The acceptance of this report, it cannot be too clearly recognized, commits this Church, as far as this representative body can commit it, to nothing less than a complete social reconstruction. . . . we think it is clear that nothing less than the goal we have outlined will satisfy the aroused moral consciousness of the Church or retain for the Church any leadership in the testing period that is upon them." The report concluded by exhorting ministers and members to familiarize themselves with recent literature on reconstruction, including the British Labour party's programme, and called for a national conference of Christian churches to consider the problems of reconstruction.[79]

The committee included most of the leading social gospellers in the church.[80] Its report was accepted by the conference with only four dissenting votes after a vigorous debate which included denunciations of the document as committing the church to socialism.[81] The fact that there was such a debate shows that the conference knew the implications of the document. The Methodist Church did not move to the left in a fit of absence of mind. To underline its concern the conference went on to accept the report of the Committee on Social Service and Evangelism which condemned unearned wealth and all forms of profiteering and recommended old age pensions, a living wage, and nationalization of excess profits, natural resources, the means of communication and transportation, and public utilities.[82]

This was the consequence of the interaction of the wartime experience with Methodism's social consciousness. One of the three largest and wealthiest Protestant denominations in Canada, only recently "in the pocket" of the Union government, had committed itself to a political and economic programme far to the left of anything acceptable to the major political parties. It was useless to charge that the church had gone socialist: "Whatever else it may mean, one thing is sure, it certainly means Christianity in practice."[83]

The Methodist Church freely and fully supported the Canadian war effort. Pacifists within the church did not significantly affect its position. Demographic factors such as national origin, residence, and education explain the church's difficulties in its recruiting drive. Zeal for the purity of Methodist sons did have an incidental effect on recruiting, but in this case the operative motive was revulsion against London bars and brothels, not revulsion against warfare.

The church supported the war because it believed the cause was just. Methodists, like most English-speaking Canadians, were "taken in" by the atrocity stories. World War II has surely taught historians to have more tolerance for people who believed atrocity stories in the earlier war. At the same time historians must ignore some of the lessons

[79]*Journal of Proceedings, Tenth Conference*, pp. 290–3.

[80]Internal evidence suggests that the report was written by either Salem Bland or Ernest Thomas.

[81]*Christian Guardian*, Oct. 23, 1918.

[82]*Journal of Proceedings, Tenth Conference*, p. 312.

[83]*Christian Guardian*, Nov. 13, 1918, editorial.

of the two wars. Most Canadians of his generation would have agreed with Dr. Chown's later statement that in 1914 "war appeared to be something legitimate, noble and even sublime."[84] Brought up in Kingston, S. D. Chown had hired a soldier's son to teach him the rudiments of drill when he was twelve years old, had enlisted in a battalion of riflemen at fifteen, and had seen active service at seventeen during the last of the Fenian raids.[85] In 1914 most Canadians shared his Fenian raid concept of war.

Paradoxically, the pacifism at the heart of the Christian gospel was largely responsible for the extremism of Methodism's defence of Canadian liberty. No Methodist could fight a war that Jesus would not have supported. Therefore Methodists could fight only a holy war. If men were not dying for Christ their deaths would have appeared to be meaningless. The despair and sorrow would have mounted with the casualties until the church would have damned the war completely. In its crusading zeal the Methodist Church acquiesced in suppressions of basic liberties; to its own people it eventually denied the right of conscience. The amount of damage that would have been done to the nation's collective morale if its religious institutions had stood in critical judgment of the war is impossible to calculate.

It is not sufficient to explain the church's wartime behaviour as a response to political and social pressures. The church was afraid of being labelled disloyal, particularly on the recruiting issue, and of the consequences for Methodism when the soldiers came home. But at the basis of this fear was the feeling that such a label would have been *justly* applied if the church had shirked its patriotic and its Christian duty. The pressures on Methodism inherent in its own theology were of greater consequence in shaping its outlook than the pressures applied by the government or by Canadian society. Coincidently they worked in the same direction.

If Methodism had been concerned either consciously or unconsciously with social status it would never have turned so radically to the left in 1918, adopting as it did a policy which must have infuriated the "pillars" of a number of its most powerful urban churches. The adoption of socialism grew directly out of the church's desire to redeem the Canadian people and the lessons it drew from the government's wartime controls. Church leaders observed the direction of government policy, thought that it was resulting in efficient and equitable allocation of resources, and concluded that such a policy was necessary for the future. In this way the war acted as a positive catalyst on Methodism's

[84]Chown Papers, undated address (postwar), "What Does the Bible Teach About War?"
[85]*Ibid.*, Both Chown and Creighton became professed pacifists in the 1920s and apologized in print for their 1914–1918 activities.

social thought, hastening the church along a path it may have been bound to take, but not a path calculated to win the maximum of public favour.

Canadian church historians have not yet noticed this aspect of the war's impact on Methodism. H. H. Walsh, the only ecclesiastical historian who has covered this period, feels that the war put the social problem into the background. He sees it raised again only by the Winnipeg general strike and finds the first signs of the rejection of personal evangelism as a method of reform appearing in the United Church's 1932 general council.[86] J. S. Woodsworth's biographer has noted the importance of the social gospel in Canada, but takes the social gospel out of Methodism along with Woodsworth and Ivens.[87] The most recent writer, Stewart Crysdale, agrees that the war caused an outburst of social idealism in Canada, but then suggests that "the disliked regimentation of the First World War and extreme disapproval of bolshevism produced a reaction in favour of individualism."[88] Nothing is more certain about the Methodists than that they liked the regimentation, such as it was, of World War I. They also thought that socialism was the best means of staving off bolshevism.[89] Crysdale himself goes on to show that the Methodist Church strongly supported labour in the postwar struggles; its radicalism was finally tempered only by church union.[90]

Another neglected problem is the connection between the social gospel and the more traditional methods of rooting out evil in Canadian life that churchmen favoured. It cannot be lightly assumed that Christian concern for temperance, sabbatarianism, and sexual restraint meant that churches were ignoring social problems to concentrate on healing flaws in individual behaviour. The Lord's Day Act of 1906 was one of the most significant extensions of the state's power to regulate social conditions made in the Laurier period. For two generations before

[86]H. H. Walsh, *The Christian Church in Canada* (Toronto, 1958), pp. 334ff.

[87]"When A. R. M. Lower suggests that Methodism fathered a large proportion of Canada's radicals perhaps he should have written 'expelled' rather than 'fathered.'" McNaught, *A Prophet in Politics*, p. 98. In 1918 there was obviously a place in the Methodist Church for the radicalism of Woodsworth and Ivens. By 1922, when the church began to repent of its support for the war, there was also a place for their pacifism. The real problem by then was that neither of them would have been willing to work again within the framework of organized religion. But other socialists, such as Ernest Thomas and Salem Bland, worked effectively in the Methodist Church and the United Church throughout the interwar years.

[88]Stewart Crysdale, *The Industrial Struggle and Protestant Ethics in Canada* (Toronto, 1961), p. xii.

[89]See, for example, the *Christian Guardian*, Nov. 6, 1918: "It has been clearly manifested that the truest safeguard against Bolshevism . . . lies not in the intellectual and social enslavement of the masses, but in their complete intellectual and social emancipation."

[90]Crysdale, *The Industrial Struggle*, pp. 76ff.

World War I Protestant churches had been applying political pressure in every conceivable form to win temperance legislation. Sabbatarians and temperance advocates aimed at creating an ideal Canadian community. They believed they were attacking the most basic social evils in Canada. Well before 1914 they had agreed that government authority was to be a main agent of social change. Because they accepted this view Methodists were sympathetic to regulation and regimentation during the war and favoured massive expansion of state power in peacetime. Social gospel thought, at least in the Methodist Church, *evolved* out of Methodism's historic concern for a just and righteous social order. It did not *supersede* an irresponsible puritanism. By 1914 the church was willing to use the state to remake the individual's life. By 1918 it was willing to use the state to remake the community. The distinction is very fine.

It may be generally true that when Canadian historians come to study the wartime experience in depth they will find that these were vital years in Canada's social and intellectual development as well as in its rise to nationhood. The new sense of identity fostered among English Canadians by the war was more than simple patriotism. It was an expression of revived ideals of service to a common principle, participation in communal activity, and membership in an organic whole. Nationalists and social reformers alike had protested against the fragmentation of community life and the destruction of spiritual values caused by rapid economic growth before the war. Because they aspired to the same end—the achievement of some form of organic unity in society—many nationalists and social reformers could unite in hailing the wartime experience as marking the birth of a new society. Indeed, as the Methodist experience demonstrates, it was both possible and consistent for the same individuals to combine militant nationalism with a determination to reconstruct Canadian society. As nationalists, as socialists, above all as Christian idealists, Methodists in 1918 were ready to participate in the creation of a peacetime community as unified and egalitarian as the wartime society. It is surprising how many other Canadians shared their determination.[91] Somewhere in the 1920s, though, the new society got lost.

[91] Significant expressions of this idealism can be found in the Farmers' platform of 1918, the Liberal party platform of 1919, the collection of essays *The New Era in Canada* (Toronto, 1917), W. L. M. King, *Industry and Humanity* (Toronto, 1918), Stephen Leacock, *The Unsolved Riddle of Social Justice* (Toronto, 1920), and C. W. Gordon ("Ralph Connor"), *To Him That Hath* (Toronto, 1921).

Registration, Conscription, and Independent Labour Politics, 1916-1917

MARTIN ROBIN

THE RESISTANCE OF ORGANIZED LABOUR to Canada's First World War effort has been scarcely considered by historians. The strains on Canadian unity arising from the war mobilization have been seen in sectional rather than class terms with Quebec nationalism providing the major exception to a war effort patriotically endorsed by all classes and regions of English-speaking Canada. Labour radicalism in English-speaking Canada has been interpreted as a postwar phenomenon, an afterthought, a product of the reconstruction period and the final months of the war, a resistance following the major war effort in 1917–18. Yet there is little support for the assumption that organized labour quietly and patriotically acquiesced to the sacrifices imposed by the war crisis. Labour leaders did not stoically accept the subordination of the "cherished fruits of agitation and organization" to "imperative war necessities."[1] From the very beginning, there was manifest a strong resistance to the war regimentation, a resistance which culminated in fierce opposition to conscription and in the entry of the Trades and Labor Congress into independent politics in opposition to the Union government.

Before Canada experienced the full impact of the war, the Trades and Labor Congress of Canada contented itself with passing resolutions declaring that wars were fought purely in the interests of the capitalists and that since the capitalists waged wars, it was their duty to do the fighting. A resolution was passed as early as 1911 at the Calgary convention supporting a general strike to prevent the outbreak of war, "so that the workers may see the pitiful exhibition of fighting of those

[1]*Canadian Annual Review*, 1917, p. 416.

Reprinted from *Canadian Historical Review*, XLVII (2), June, 1966

capitalists who seem so fond of it."[2] A year later the Congress reiterated its opposition to war: "the only result that a war between Germany and Great Britain would achieve would be the degradation of the toilers."[3] There was a slight modification of this stand at the Montreal convention when Congress policy again opposed participation in an international war but acknowledged it was "not a war of Great Britain's choosing." The executive was determined that "despotism in Europe will be hurled to its final destruction, to make way for constitutional freedom in all the countries in Europe, in preparation for the last and great struggle of the working class for their own actual freedom."[4] At the Saint John convention the question was again judiciously disposed of. When the Congress met in Vancouver in 1915, previous resolutions opposing war in principle were endorsed, but the executive council threw down the gauntlet to the militant socialists who maintained that the war was no business of the working class and that it was therefore a matter of indifference which side won. Voluntary assistance was pledged as a part of a "mighty endeavour to secure early and final victory for the cause of freedom and democracy."[5] But compulsion in any form was opposed. The recommendation of the executive committee calling for "unchangeable opposition to all that savours of conscription either here or in the empire" was unanimously endorsed.[6] The anti-conscription resolution was reaffirmed the following year.[7]

The determination of Canadian labour to resist the halting move of the Borden government towards the registration and conscription of manpower was put to a severe test during the years 1916–17. In April, 1916, influential sections of the Canadian population asked for registration of the nation's manpower and resources and for government action in the redistribution and allotment of the workers for services "voluntary, yet selective."[8] A large deputation representing recruiting leagues interviewed the Prime Minister and presented a memorial calling for conscription beginning with registration. At a conference of these representatives in Ottawa, the Canadian Service League was born.[9]

[2]*Labour Gazette*, XII, 344.   [3]*Ibid.*, XIII, 352.

[4]Canada, Department of Labour, *Fourth Annual Report on Labour Organization in Canada*, 1914, p. 20.

[5]*Proceedings of the 31st Annual Convention of the Trades and Labor Congress of Canada*, 1915, p. 14.

[6]*Ibid.*, pp. 15, 91.

[7]*Proceedings of the 32nd Annual Convention of the Trades and Labor Congress of Canada*, 1916, p. 23.

[8]*Canadian Annual Review*, 1916, pp. 318–24. A number of National Service Leagues were formed to press the government for registration.

[9]Chief Justice Mather of Winnipeg was appointed honorary president. The purpose of the association was "to promote any form of National Service which the need of the hour may demand." *Ibid.*

The increasing pressure for National Service was soon felt within the T.L.C. President Watters sent out a circular on April 29, 1916, asking the various affiliated central trades councils and unions whether they were willing to endorse the Vancouver resolution calling for "unchangeable opposition to all that savours of conscription." Watters also sounded the unions on the advisability of calling a general strike: "To prevent anything that savours of 'conscription' . . . are you prepared if every other means should fail, to use the most effective and almost the only weapon within your reach. . . . Or should occasion require it, are you prepared to simply register a protest?"[10]

In August, 1916, the government passed an Order-in-Council authorizing the appointment of a National Service Board with general power of supervision over security and labour selection. A Director-General of National Service was appointed, charged with the duty of directing and co-ordinating the work of the directors of National Service to be appointed in each military district.[11] R. B. Bennett, the newly appointed Director-General met with his directors in November and devised plans for an inventory of Canadian manpower. Bennett and his colleagues decided to distribute a series of registration cards to be filled out by workers throughout the dominion in order to gather basic information as to manpower location and distribution.

The proposed registration scheme did not sit well with some sections of organized labour. The industrial element of Canada was deeply affected by this call for service, yet organized labour was granted no representation on the National Service Board. Indeed the leaders of organized labour were not even consulted before the step was taken.[12] Labour leaders feared that employers would use the registration movement for the purpose of interfering with union labour and establishing an open shop. It was strongly felt too that behind registration was an intention on the part of the government to bring in conscription.

Organized labour's growing fears were expressed at a series of meetings at which the Prime Minister and Director-General spoke on behalf of the National Service Board of Canada for the purpose of enlisting "the active support and sympathy of the people."[13] Borden and Bennett toured the country from Montreal to Victoria in December. The

[10]*Industrial Banner*, May 5, 1916.

[11]Public Archives of Canada, Borden Papers, OC313(2) 34674, National Service resolution as established by Order-in-Council, Oct. 5, 1916. The duty of the directors of National Service was to find out the number of men who could be removed from the various industries carried out in any locality within each district and to provide that no person be allowed to enlist "whose services would be of more value to the state in the employment in which he is now engaged."

[12]*Ibid.*, H. H. Stevens to R. B. Bennett, Dec. 20, 1916.

[13]*Ibid.*, OC 313(43) 35016.

speakers met with particularly strong opposition in Winnipeg and in the west coast province. Borden had been warned before his departure by H. H. Stevens about labour unrest on the coast.[14] As early as December 11, James McVety, president of the British Columbia Federation of Labor, had written James Watters asking for information regarding the powers of the Registration Commission and Watters' reply indicated that he had very little information and had been unable to secure copies of the Order-in-Council creating the Commission.[15] Watters suggested that the British Columbia labour men interview the Prime Minister when he came to the coast,[16] and a meeting was arranged in Vancouver. Vice-presidents Morrison and Yates and Secretary Victor Midgley of the Vancouver Trades and Labor Council accompanied McVety. The delegation sought an assurance from Borden and Bennett that conscription would not be instituted. No assurance was forthcoming. Following the interview, a joint meeting of the coast officials of the Federation and the executive committees of the trades councils of Victoria and Vancouver was held, at which the delegates presented their unanimous opposition to the registration proposal.[17]

Following the tour, Borden and Bennett met with the leading Congress officials in Ottawa. The Congress executive asked for an assurance that under no circumstances would conscription be undertaken or carried out.[18] Borden again declined. He expressed the hope that conscription would not be necessary but "if it should prove the only effective method to preserve the existence of the state and of the institutions and liberties which we enjoy I should consider it necessary and I should not hesitate to act accordingly."[19] To the complaints that burdens and sacrifices were being unequally distributed, Borden replied that "the government accepted and acted on the principle that the accumulated wealth of the country should bear its due proportion of contributions and sacrifices in the war." Any further proposals would first have to be submitted to parliament after obtaining the sanction and approval of the government. Despite Borden's failure to disavow manpower conscription, or support the conscription of wealth, the Congress executive issued circulars to all labour unions following the

[14]*Ibid.*, Stevens to R. L. Borden, Dec. 22, 1916. Stevens impressed on him "the imperative necessity of winning the confidence of the labour men of Canada by recognition and consultation."

[15]*Ibid.*, Stevens to Bennett, Dec. 20, 1916. Stevens noted that Watters had not been extended the courtesy of being sent copies of the Order-in-Council.

[16]*British Columbia Federationist*, Jan. 12, 1917.

[17]*Ibid.*

[18]Borden Papers, Borden to J. C. Watters, James Simpson, and R. A. Rigg, Dec. 27, 1916.   [19]*Ibid.*

meeting urging their co-operation in making National Service Week a success.[20]

The executive recommendation met with agreement in the east, and a storm of protest throughout the west. James Simpson attended meetings of the Toronto and Hamilton trades councils and testified to assurances given by Borden.[21] The trades councils of Toronto, Ottawa, Hamilton, Guelph, Saint John, Peterborough and St. Catharines supported the executive recommendation.[22] But western labour leaders bitterly opposed both the registration measure and the recommendation of the Congress executive. On December 21, 1916, the Winnipeg Trades and Labor Council took the lead and appointed a committee to oppose registration. President Harry Veitch openly declared he would not sign the National Service cards. The *Voice* echoed the sentiments of the central labour council delegates when it warned against registration as a prelude to conscription which "would bring the worker to heel, depriving him of the right of collective bargaining and forcing him to accept whatever terms might be offered."[23] An anti-registration committee was formed by the central bodies in Winnipeg and Transcona. The Winnipeg Trades and Labor Council recommended that the cards not be signed.[24]

The New Westminster, Victoria, and Vancouver central councils also served notice to the Congress executive of their opposition to the registration scheme, considering it a step towards conscription. At a meeting on January 4, the Vancouver council emphatically expressed itself as opposed to the National Service scheme and reiterated the demand that wealth be conscripted and basic industries nationalized.[25] The central councils of Victoria, Regina, and Saskatoon reaffirmed their opposition and the Calgary council called for a special Trades and Labor Congress convention to consider the matter.[26] At the Revelstoke convention of the British Columbia Federation of Labor in January, the delegates went on record against registration and conscription and censured the executive of the T.L.C. for violation of the expressed opinion of the last convention.[27] It further demanded that conscription not be put into effect before the matter had been

[20]The notice was signed by J. C. Watters, James Simpson, P. M. Draper, and R. A. Rigg. Dated Dec. 28, it recommended that "all members of affiliated unions fill in the answers according to their conscientious opinion and return the cards as directed." *Sixth Annual Report on Labour Organization in Canada*, 1916, pp. 39–40.

[21]*Industrial Banner*, Jan. 12, 1917, p. 2.

[22]*Sixth Annual Report on Labour Organization in Canada*, 1916, pp. 45–6.

[23]The *Voice*, Dec. 29, 1916.

[24]*Canadian Forward*, Jan. 13, 1917.

[25]*British Columbia Federationist*, Feb. 19, 1917.

[26]*Sixth Annual Report on Labour Organization in Canada*, 1916, pp. 41–5.

[27]*British Columbia Federationst*, Feb. 19, 1917.

submitted to a referendum and that electoral reforms be introduced to widen the franchise. President J. H. McVety bitterly criticized Watters for selling out to the Borden régime and Watters accused McVety of "planting the germs of sectional differences in the minds of the workers."[28] At a meeting of the Winnipeg Central Trades and Labor Council in January the local delegates reaffirmed their opposition to registration, recommended that the workers not fill out the cards, and severely censured the dominion executive for supporting registration.[29] Congress President Watters considered the action of the Winnipeg council as "not only inexplicable, but deplorable."[30]

When Sir Robert Borden announced on May 18, 1917, that conscription was imperative, the worst fears of the western labour radicals were confirmed. The Alberta Federation of Labour, which claimed the affiliation of 70 local unions and represented 7,000 workers, adopted a resolution protesting the conscription of manpower until the wealth of the nation had first been conscripted.[31] At a special meeting of the Vancouver Trades and Labor Council on May 30, the delegates voted by a 90 per cent majority to resist "by any means" in their power the passage of a conscription law and instructed the executive of the British Columbia Federation of Labor to take an immediate referendum regarding the calling of a general strike in the province in the event of the passage of a conscription law. Mass protest meetings, addressed by members of the Socialist party of Canada, were held throughout the province and on June 13 a meeting was held in the Empress Theatre in Vancouver under the joint auspices of the Socialist party of Canada and the Trades and Labor Council.[32] The executive committee of the British Columbia Federation of Labor submitted a proposal to the membership throughout the province to down tools in the event of conscription,[33] and in August voted unanimously to call a special convention of the provincial body to consider the results of the general strike referendum and to plan the future course of action. The convention met on September 1 when it was announced that the referendum had passed by a large 5 to 1 majority. The delegates voted, however, to keep the down tools policy in abeyance. The executive was given full power to call a general strike should it deem the course imperative. A strong recommendation for political action passed by a large majority.[34]

The Trades and Labor Councils of Victoria, Trail, and New Westminster reacted the same way as the Vancouver council and the

28Ibid., Jan. 5, 1917.
29The Voice, Jan. 5, 1917.   30Ibid.
31Seventh Annual Report on Labour Organization in Canada, 1917, p. 31.
32British Columbia Federationist, June 1 and June 15, 1917.
33Ibid., June 8, 1917.   34Ibid., Sept. 7, 1917.

provincial federation and passed heated resolutions against conscription as did the Prince Rupert council which declared for the conscription of wealth production before the conscription of manpower. The Lethbridge, Winnipeg, and Medicine Hat councils all entered emphatic protests.[35] The Calgary council joined in the opposition and heard the Reverend William Irvine argue that "every man should give up his bank book and all he had before men should be forced to fight."[36] The Winnipeg council adopted a resolution on May 31 against conscription and demanded that the question be submitted to the people as a referendum. A vote of the affiliated unions on the question of a general strike, provided similar action was adopted in all other cities, was later taken, and out of 54 unions supplied with ballots returns were received from 23, the result being 1,787 in favour and 736 against.[37]

Ontario labour leaders were equally adamant. They had supported the Congress executive's recommendation not to oppose registration, but now stood strongly opposed to the conscription of manpower without the conscription of wealth. Soon after Borden's announcement of the conscription measure, the Toronto Trades and Labor Council passed a resolution in favour of the conscription of wealth with manpower.[38] The Ottawa, Kitchener, Guelph, and South Waterloo councils urged the conscription of all sources of wealth while the London council demanded the "nationalization of all the resources of the Dominion."[39] The central councils in Niagara Falls, Brantford, and Sault Ste Marie also opposed conscription. At a meeting on May 25 of the Ontario Labour Educational Association, the only province-wide federation of trade unions and central labour councils in Ontario, resolutions were passed favouring the nationalization of "the industries in the country which are necessary to the successful carrying out of the War—the wages and conditions of the workers to be guaranteed by the government" and nationalization of the banks of Canada.[40]

The strong opposition to the proposed conscription measure met with the support of the Congress executive. Friction and differences between the west and the executive over the registration question were momentarily forgotten. In January President Watters believed that opposition to registration was based on the erroneous assumption that it was only a preliminary step to conscription such as had taken place in Great Britain.[41] He argued that there was a wide difference between

[35]*Seventh Annual Report on Labour Organization in Canada*, 1917, p. 32.
[36]*Canadian Annual Review*, 1917, p. 419.
[37]*Seventh Annual Report on Labour Organization in Canada*, 1917, p. 32.
[38]*Ibid.*   [39]*Ibid.*
[40]*Canadian Annual Review*, 1917, p. 419.
[41]*British Columbia Federationist*, Feb. 16, 1917.

the system adopted in Great Britain and in Canada. "The system of registration put into operation in Great Britain led to conscription, the system of registration in Canada is designed to lead away from conscription."[42] He therefore maintained that the Order-in-Council appointing the board and defining its duties conflicted in no particular way with the war policy of the Congress.[43] But with conscription imminent, Watters mended the error of his ways and placed himself at the head of the mounting protest. He was supported by Simpson.[44] Watters, Simpson, and Draper met with Borden in the prime minister's office on May 21 to hear a statement in justification of his recent declaration in favour of "the Selective Conscription of between 50,000 and 100,000 men to preserve complete the four Battalions of Canadian soldiers overseas."[45] They demanded that the conscription measure not be put through and that labour be given representation in the cabinet. Vice-President Simpson told the Prime Minister that "no other country had treated organized labour with such scant courtesy," to which Borden replied that a start had been made towards a fitting recognition of organized labour by appointing a labour man to the Senate.[46] The executive council of the T.L.C. shortly thereafter summoned a meeting of 80 international trade unions including the Railway Brotherhoods and the Federation of Letter Carriers. The convention met June 1 to 4 and demanded drastic changes in the conduct of the war.[47]

The *Industrial Banner* happily noted that organized labour was no longer talking to the Ottawa government in whispers.[48] Representatives of the machinists, carpenters, plumbers and steamfitters, sheet metal workers, and many other organizations declared that the wages and conditions of labour on the work under the control of the Imperial Munitions Board were a scandal and a disgrace.[49] J. W. Flavelle and C. S. Gordon were declared to be absolutely unfair and antagonistic

[42]*Ibid.*

[43]*Ibid.* According to Watters the opposite was the case since the registration plan had for its avowed purpose the taking stock of the material requirements of food, munitions, and all other measures including labour (manpower) requisite for securing "an early and final victory for the cause of freedom and democracy," without resorting to compulsory methods. The manifest duty of the executive under the circumstances therefore had been to recommend support.

[44]Secretary Draper was silent on conscription and was not opposed. *British Columbia Federationist,* June 8, 1917.

[45]*Proceedings of the 33rd Annual Convention of the Trades and Labor Congress of Canada,* 1917, p. 36.

[46]*Ibid.,* p. 40. Gideon Robertson, a vice-president of the Brotherhood of Railway Telegraphers, had been appointed to the Senate in 1917 as a concession to labour. The *Labor News* (Feb. 2, 1917) described him as "a big good-looking clean shaven Canadian, one of the statesmen among the ranks of the railway labor officials."

[47]*British Columbia Federationist,* June 15, 1917.

[48]*Industrial Banner,* June 8, 1917.

[49]*Ibid.*

to the workers. Their public attitude was condemned as cant and hypocrisy.[50] Borden was described as going around with the Bible under one arm and the complete plans and specifications for the robbery of the country under the other.[51] The delegates declared themselves emphatically opposed to the proposed conscription measure and urged the workers to oppose "by every means in their power the enactment of such legislation."[52] Only five members of the entire delegation opposed the statement, three of whom qualified their opposition by declaring that along with the conscription of manpower must come the conscription of wealth.[53] The joint committee composed of the Congress executive and representatives of the Railway Brotherhoods reported an intense feeling that "the time of petitioning the government is about passed, and action throughout the country by organized labour is necessary and that now is the time to decide what to do."[54]

Following the conference, Vice-President Simpson advised that steps be taken to form an organization of workmen's and soldiers' councils similar to the soviets in Russia.[55] Alphonse Verville, Liberal-Labour member for Maisonneuve told the House of Commons on June 28 that a general strike was possible.[56] James Watters demanded nationalization of the mines, railways, munitions works, and other establishments necessary for the prosecution of the war including the banking system and warned the organized workers not to permit themselves to be shackled with the chains of conscription. On July 15, Watters addressed 3,000 anti-war French Canadians at Hull and declared that on the day the Military Service Act passed "organized labour would lay down its tools and refuse to work." He denounced Lloyd George as "a tricky politician who had disgraced humanity," criticized Sir J. W. Flavelle, and declared that "we must, and shall, refuse to be sent to the Front to protect profiteers."[57] The T.L.C. president favoured a national general strike to force the government to conscript wealth as well as manpower. While the British Columbia Federation of Labor was taking a vote on the general strike question, Secretary Wells wrote Watters on the subject of "ulterior measures." Watters replied,

I am strongly of the opinion then, that the greatest and most patriotic service we can render to our country, our mother-land, and our allies in the struggle to preserve our liberties and our democracy, is, on the day conscription of manpower is put into effect, to implement the pledge of the prime minister by forcing the government to conscript material wealth through every worker in the Dominion

---

[50]*Ibid.*　　　　　　　　　　　　　　　　[51]*Ibid.*
[52]*Canadian Annual Review,* 1917, p. 419.
[53]*Industrial Banner,* June 8, 1917.　　　　[54]*Ibid.*
[55]*Canadian Annual Review,* 1917, p. 417.
[56]*Ibid.,* p. 420.　　　　　　　　　　　　[57]*Ibid.*

refusing to work for the gain of the private profiteer and offering his service to the nation, and the nation alone. In other words not a wheel of industry would turn save only for the nation in its hour of need. . . .[58]

Lest he be misunderstood, Watters explained further:

Let labor demonstrate their loyalty and patriotism on the day manpower is conscripted by seeing that the work of their brain and every ounce of their physical energy is utilized for the support of the men at the front, and in defence of the nation, to provide ample remuneration and adequate pensions to the men in khaki and a full measure of protection to the dependents of such men and to relieve the nation from the burden of debt which the productive work of labour can meet—even if a general strike is necessary to bring it about.[59]

The question of a national general strike was considered at the Trades and Labor Congress convention in September. Conscription was already the law of the land and the War-time Elections Act had passed the House of Commons in preparation for the approaching federal election. The Ottawa convention became the forum for a bitter debate on "ulterior measures." The growing split between east and west, between the supporters of "political" and "direct" action, was readily apparent. The temper of the western delegates was revealed on the first day when Delegate Naylor, the president of the coast provincial federation, rose on a question of privilege when President J. Cameron of the Trades and Labor Council in Ottawa invited the Hon. T. W. Crothers, the Minister of Labour, to the platform. Naylor pointed out, to the delight of his western compeers, that Crothers was not on the schedule of speakers and insisted it would be a waste of time to hear him. He said that the delegates had heard him before and knew what he would say.[60] Crothers later addressed a stone-silent audience.

The great debate was initiated when the Committee on Officers Reports recommended the adoption of the executive's recommendation on conscription which read as follows:

While the Congress cannot stultify itself to the degree of either withdrawing or contradicting this year its firm and carefully thought out views on the question of Conscription, as embodied in the Resolutions of 1915 and 1916, still, under our representative form of Government it is not deemed either right, patriotic or in the interests of the Dominion or of the Labor classes to say or do aught that might prevent the powers that be from obtaining all the results that they anticipate from the enforcement of such law.[61]

Western delegates, along with those from Quebec and a few Ontario socialists, bitterly attacked the report as an easy surrender to state

[58]The *Voice*, July 6, 1917.   [59]*Ibid.*
[60]*Proceedings of the 33rd Annual Convention of the Trades and Labor Congress of Canada*, 1917, p. 4.   [61]*Ibid.*, p. 43.

tyranny. Delegate Farmilo of Edmonton sought to amend it with a proposal that the government conscript wealth before manpower and that pending the conscription of wealth, no support be given to the principle of conscripting men for war purposes.[62] Speaking in support of the Farmilo amendment, Vice-President Simpson noted that the government had disregarded entirely the interests of the workers of the country in the discussion of the war programme and declared that organized labour was hardly satisfied with the government's claim to have fulfilled its obligations towards labour by the appointment of a senator from the ranks of organized labour—"No member of organized labor appointed to the Senate by either the Liberal or Conservative Government is free to serve the working class as they should be served in the Upper Chamber, and therefore, in my judgement, the action of the Government cannot be regarded as a concession to labor."[63] The Farmilo direct action amendment lost by 10 votes, 111 to 101. Other amendments on the same subject met with a similar fate. Delegate Arcand from Quebec called for pressure to force a postponement of the enactment of the law until election time. Delegate Bruce advocated outright opposition to the Act and a Congress pledge to work for its repeal. By a vote of 134 to 101 the executive's report passed with minor amendments. With few exceptions, the delegates from Winnipeg and points west opposed it and demanded "ulterior measures."

The rejection of direct action did not mean the Congress executive favoured inaction. The central thesis of the executive report was that conscription was the law of the land and the laws could not and should not be changed by direct action either in the form of a general strike or by passive resistance. Watters and Simpson had spoken very seriously during the summer of the utility of a general strike. They now shared with other members of the executive the view that political action was the only sensible course.[64] Labour leaders had earlier called for a referendum on conscription and other war measures: the general election would in fact act as the referendum.

Resuming where the Congress left off in 1906, the executive recommended and the delegates endorsed the formation of a national labour party to contest the approaching federal election and express labour's opposition to the war policy of the Borden régime. The executive acknowledged that earlier plunges into independent politics had not

[62]*Ibid.*, p. 142.   [63]*Ibid.*, p. 154.
[64]The *Voice* adequately summed up the position. "Conscription is the law of the land, until the people declare that it is a law they do not want. The election which is coming is to decide the fate of this law and determine whether it shall remain. It is for the people to decide." As quoted in the *British Columbia Federationist*, Aug. 31, 1917.

resulted in the construction of "a harmonious and virile workers' political organization."[65] It recommended the British Labour party precedent and plan of organization which allowed for group affiliation and the contracting out of individual members. Only through group affiliation and contracting out would it be possible to "recognize the liberty of the individual to accept a varied programme of working class political action and at the same time to unite on a cooperative basis to build up a political organization that will give effect to the fundamental principles underlying the legislative demands of the workers."[66]

The executive's recommendation represented a new attempt to heal the schisms of past years. It went a step further than the earlier one of 1906 when the executive had refused to recognize existing socialist organizations as the legitimate expression of the labour movement and had sought to create a straight labour party independent of and, in British Columbia, opposed to the socialists.[67] The new emphasis was on the co-operation and recognition of "organizations having similar objectives as those affiliated with the British Labour Party." Socialists, trade unionists, farmers, and other progressives were invited to sink their differences in a new partnership.[68] The "dominating political organization" in each province was urged to call a conference of "the respective organizations entitled to partnership in such a Labour Party and proceed to cooperate for political action."[69]

The main support for direct action came from the Winnipeg and Pacific Coast unions. The initiative for political action came from Ontario. Western radicals were not opposed to political action. The leading coast unions had supported it at the special convention of the British Columbia Federation of Labor in September. But, like the Winnipeg unionists, they were equally determined to play with the general strike idea. Both political action and direct action were endorsed at the British Columbia provincial convention as protest weapons against conscription, although the latter was to be kept in abeyance until the former had been tried. Ontario unions were uniformly opposed to a general strike protest and were optimistic about the possibilities of independent political action. By 1917, the centre of gravity of independent labour and socialist politics had shifted from British Columbia, where it flourished preceding the war, to Ontario.[70]

[65]*Proceedings of the 33rd Annual Convention of the Trades and Labor Congress of Canada*, 1917, p. 43.
[66]*Ibid.*
[67]The T.L.C. never recognized the Socialist party of Canada, the dominant radical political party in British Columbia in pre-war years, as a "legitimate labor party."
[68]*Proceedings of the 33rd Annual Convention of the Trades and Labor Congress of Canada*, 1917, p. 43.
[69]*Ibid.*, p. 44.
[70]The Congress executive's recommendation for political action was plainly inspired

Ontario unionists were well prepared to fight the conscription election. Radical labour politics in Ontario had reached its nadir during the provincial election of 1914; by 1917, however, the province was the best organized in the dominion. The new trend was first evident when an independent labour party was formed in London in April, 1916, after several meetings and conferences at which the platforms of the Hamilton Independent Labor party, the Trades and Labor Congress of Canada, and the Independent Labour party of Great Britain were considered.[71]

Supporters of independent labour politics in London, Hamilton, and Toronto began to push their views within the Labour Educational Association, a purely voluntary organization formed in Woodstock, Ontario, in 1903 with the object "of bringing in close touch the workers throughout the province willing to cooperate to advance the principle of the labour movement and labour when and where possible."[72] Originally restricted to western Ontario, the new association expanded to include all areas of the province and provided the sole province-wide forum of union co-operation.[73] The advocates of an independent labour party made good use of the Association for propaganda and organizational purposes. Secretary-Treasurer Joseph Marks, a strong supporter of independent politics, edited the *Industrial Banner*, a lively labour weekly with a wide circulation. James Simpson, Joseph Gibbons, and T. A. Stevenson were all members of the executive board of the paper, and joined with Marks in supporting the new movement.[74] The *Industrial Banner* soon became the leading propaganda agency for the new party. It published weekly front-page articles urging independent political action. Simpson, Marks, and Stevenson toured the province on a lecture circuit sponsored by the Association. They were joined by Laura Hughes, the niece of Sir Sam Hughes, who had electrified the delegates at the 1916 T.L.C. convention with a stirring radical speech.[75]

by the political activities of Ontario unionists. The executive report gladly noted the considerable activity in Ontario during the year to organize a provincial labour party and recommended the new Ontario political organization as a model. The action of the Independent Labor party of Ontario in providing for endorsation of candidates nominated by other "strictly working class organizations" was "highly commendable and suggests the possibility of organizing a National Labour Party." *Ibid.*

[71]*Industrial Banner*, Aug. 13, 1916. The chairman of the new party was J. F. Thomson, formerly a lecturer in England for the Land Nationalization Society and Alderman for Salford, near Manchester. Many of the members had been active in the British Independent Labour party and had corresponded with the I.L.P. of Hamilton, the sole remaining local of the Independent Labor party of Ontario formed in 1907.

[72]*Industrial Banner*, March 27, 1914.   [73]*Labor News*, Oct. 31, 1919.

[74]*Industrial Banner*, Dec. 8, 1916.

[75]Miss Hughes was a recent convert to the labour cause. She advocated an independent labour party as the only solution to the disgraceful employment conditions found in the armament factories she toured as an inspector.

Political unity in Toronto was achieved on November 13, 1916, when representatives of the various labour groups in Toronto met and formed the Greater Toronto Labor party.[76] An executive committee composed of 23 representatives from the constituent groups was set up. There were present fraternal delegates from Hamilton and Niagara Falls Independent Labor parties.[77] The sudden appearance of party groups in Temiskaming, Kirkland Lake, Cobalt, and North Bay testified to the organizational ability of Simpson who made a number of tours of northern Ontario. Delegates attending the fifteenth annual convention of the Labour Educational Association unanimously resolved that it give its "utmost support to the formation of branches of the Independent Labour Party throughout Ontario," and instructed secretary Marks to call a convention immediately of representatives from all the labour parties organized to meet at a central point for the purpose of forming a provincial independent labour party.[78]

The founding convention of the Ontario Independent Labor party on July 2, 1917, was attended by 16 branch locals from Cobalt, North Bay, Norwood, Toronto, Kingston, Niagara Falls, Port Colborne, Welland, Thorold, Chippewa, Hamilton, Brantford, Guelph, Kitchener, and London.[79] When the Greater Toronto Labor party was formed in November, 1916, only two other similar organizations existed in the province—in London and Hamilton. By mid-June, 1917, there were 13 local parties with seven more in the process of formation.[80] Walter Rollo of Hamilton was elected president and a six-member executive committee was set up including Laura Hughes and Marks.[81] The constitution provided for direct membership.[82] Although no member of the party could be a member of any other political organization, the convention endorsed co-operation with "other bona fide parties which are clearly not capitalist organizations." Both the U.F.O. and the Social Democratic party were formally approved. The object of the new party was "to promote the political, economic and social interests of people who live by their labour, mental or manual, as distinguished from those who live by profit upon the labour of others." The organization would act "in cooperation as far as possible with independent political organizations of the farmers and the producing class for the purpose of electing men or women who will stand by the democratic principle of a working class movement with all that the term implies."[83]

With political machinery at hand, plans to create an Ontario section of the Canadian Labor party were postponed until after the election.

[76]*Industrial Banner*, April 6, 1917.   [77]*Ibid.*, April 20, 1917.
[78]*Ibid.*, June 1, 1917.   [79]*Ibid.*, July 6, 1917.
[80]*Ibid.*, June 15, 1917.   [81]*Ibid.*, June 15, 1917.
[82]*Ibid.*, July 6, 1917.   [83]*Ibid.*, July 6, 1917.

On October 6, the executive committee of the Trades and Labor Congress of Canada for the province of Ontario received a communication from J. C. Watters that a convention be called for the purpose of starting a political party. Chairman H. J. Halford summoned a meeting of the provincial executive committee which met on October 21, 1917. Halford informed the committee that he did not think it advisable to call a convention until after the election had taken place. The committee agreed and the founding convention of the Ontario section of the Canadian Labor party was left in abeyance. The executive decided to begin correspondence with the Independent Labour, social democratic, and farmers' organizations in preparation for the convention.

The Greater Toronto Labor party contested four constituencies in the campaign, East York, East Toronto, South York, and South Toronto.[84] The candidates ran on a programme which included demands for the conscription of wealth as well as manpower, a square deal for the returned soldiers and their dependents, and the curtailment of the "policy of procrastination, graft and profiteering that has reigned unchecked while the Borden administration has been in power."[85] Other candidates ran for election in Toronto Centre, Algoma West, Brantford, Hamilton East, Hamilton West, Nipissing, Temiskaming, Welland, Wentworth, Waterloo South, Fort William and Rainy River, and Port Arthur and Kenora. In Nipissing, railwayman Charles Harrison received the I.L.P. nomination but ran unopposed by the unionists. He was later elected and sat as a Unionist. A young progressive lawyer, Arthur W. Roebuck, contested Temiskaming on a Liberal-Labor ticket.[86]

The leading figures of the new Independent Labor party took an active part in the campaign. President Walter Rollo, who contested Hamilton West, was appointed national leader of the Labor party after consultation with James Watters who earlier had been suggested for the position by the Alberta Federation of Labour.[87] Laura Hughes, A. W. Mance, and Joseph Marks addressed meetings throughout the province.[88] A formal request was submitted to Samuel Gompers by Labor party officials to release John Flett, A.F.L. organizer for Hamilton for one month for service in his home city as a labour candidate.[89] Flett did not run, but campaigned against the Union government, alleging that it

[84]Ibid., Nov. 16, 1917.   [85]Ibid., Nov. 23, 1917.
[86]Ibid. The labour candidates in Fort William, Port Arthur and Kenora, Toronto East, and Hamilton East also ran unopposed by the Liberals.
[87]Ibid. Rollo initially supported Watters as leader because of his permanent residence in Ottawa. They conferred and decided that Rollo should fill the position. Watters spoke in support of the party.
[88]James Simpson was on a temperance tour of the empire during the campaign.
[89]Industrial Banner, Nov. 23, 1917.

had not taken labour into its confidence as was the case in Great Britain and the United States. Gompers and A.F.L. Secretary Morrison, a Canadian by birth, spoke at the armouries in Toronto in late November in support of the war effort and Union government.[90] The A.F.L. president's first act upon arrival in the city was to apply for $10,000 worth of victory bonds in the name of the A.F.L. upon which he made a 10 per cent deposit.[91] He spoke of the prominent part that organized labour in the United States was taking in the war and referred to the gallantry of the Canadian soldiers at the front and the admiration with which their triumphs on "the blood-stained fields of Flanders" were hailed in America. He claimed that labour should recognize that a war was on with the cause of democracy at stake. It was up to labour to back the government in every effort to win the war.[92]

In Winnipeg, R. S. Ward and R. A. Rigg, who resigned his seat in the provincial legislature, contested Winnipeg Centre and Winnipeg North as representatives of the newly-formed Manitoba section of the Canadian Labor party.[93] Both candidates were nominated at a convention of 600 attended by representatives of the Labour Representation Committee, Social Democratic party, Socialist party of Canada, the People's Council, and Single Taxers.[94] They ran unopposed by the Liberals. There were current rumours in the press that Samuel Gompers would be brought to Winnipeg to campaign against Rigg and Ward. "Gompers might as well be told" the *British Columbia Federationist* editorialized, "that the labour movement in Canada requires none of the sort of assistance that he is intellectually qualified to give."[95]

The political activists in British Columbia decided to continue the policy announced at the special convention of the British Columbia Federation of Labor in September. The provincial federation assumed the functions of a political party and nominated, sponsored, and financed independent candidates. On October 9, at a convention of labour delegates, James McVety was nominated without opposition to contest Vancouver South, and V. R. Midgley to run in Burrard.[96] Following the prescription of the September convention not to oppose Socialist party candidates already in the field, no labour candidate was nominated in Vancouver Centre where W. A. Pritchard was already in the field. The Vancouver nomination meeting was called to order by McVety, vice-president of the British Columbia Federation of Labor.

[90]*Ibid.*   [91]*Ibid.*   [92]*Ibid.*
[93]*Manitoba Free Press,* Nov. 8, 1917.
[94]*Winnipeg Telegram,* Nov. 20, 1917.
[95]As quoted in the *Voice,* Dec. 21, 1917. Andrew McBeth, a Liberal-Labour candidate, ran in Regina while Joseph Knight ran as a socialist in Red Deer.
[96]*British Columbia Federationist,* Oct. 12, 1917.

The convention unanimously adopted the platform and policy of the provincial federation. An amendment that the platform of the Trades and Labor Congress be adopted was defeated.[97] A provincial federation campaign committee was set up to finance candidates in Victoria, Nanaimo, East and West Kootenay, and Vancouver. Candidates A. S. Wells, Victor Midgley, and James McVety were all officials of the provincial organization. The election manifesto issued by the executive of the Federation made the programme of the Ontario I.L.P. look pale indeed. It included repeal of the Military Service Act, extension of the franchise to all adult citizens irrespective of sex, state care and increased benefits for soldiers and their dependents, and the abolition of the "root cause of all wars, the capitalist system."[98]

None of the Labor party candidates was returned in the election. Strong showings were made in Hamilton and Temiskaming, where labour candidates gained approximately 30 and 40 per cent respectively, of the vote.[99] But labour candidates were unable to poll more than 20 per cent of the vote in the 27 constituencies contested in English-speaking Canada and more than half of these votes went for candidates who ran unopposed by the Liberals. The "pure" independent labour and socialist candidates obtained less than 8 per cent of the popular vote in the constituencies contested. The strong showing of the Union government in the west and Ontario, in urban as well as rural areas, suggests that, despite the opposition of prominent labour leaders, a great many workers voted Unionist while others expressed their opposition to the Union government not through the Canadian Labor party but through support for the Laurier Liberals.

This is not surprising. Articulate protest against the war policies of the Union government emanated from the organized section of the working class but this group comprised only 2 per cent of the Canadian population in 1916. The Canadian labour movement was still in its infancy when Canada entered the First World War, and the high immigration rate, the mobility of the labour population, its geographical and cultural heterogeneity, and the stout resistance of the employing class kept trade unions weak and few in number. Writing in the *Voice* in 1916, H. J. Laski observed that Canadian labour had not yet discovered an "essential unity," and that only the relatively well-organized railway unions and the miners "have succeeded in inspiring that wholesome fear into the heart of capital which seems essential to progress.[100] Divsions within the working class, in skill level, income, organization,

[97]*Ibid.*   [98]*Ibid.*, Dec. 14, 1917.
[99]Results of the election are taken from Canada, *Sessional Papers* (No. 13), 1920, Vol. LVI, No. 4, *Returns of the Thirteenth General Election for the House of Commons of Canada.*
[100]The *Voice*, June 9, 1916.

and ethnic and religious affiliation prevented the emergence of a homogeneous working-class consciousness. There was clearly no labour bloc or labour vote which could be swung at will by radical spokesmen like James Watters or James Simpson and the traditional parties, Liberal and Conservative, still commanded the political affiliation of the majority of workers, from the aristrocratic Railway Brotherhoods, led by staunch conservatives like Gideon Robertson, Calvin Lawrence, and C. B. Nicholson, to the lowly unskilled labourers in the coal fields of Alberta or Vancouver Island.[101]

But the manifest failure of labour's entry into independent politics need not obscure the fact that a new mood of militancy and a spirit of independence took root as the war crisis developed. The Borden régime sought to maximize Canada's war effort through massive compulsory mobilization. The price it paid was the alienation of an increasingly articulate labour leadership in English-speaking Canada as well as the uniform loss of Quebec support. Laski wrote in June, 1916, that the Canadian labour movement was placid and led by quietists—"the leading spirits are quietists, there is little that is aggressive in the movement. It has no vivid life. Its leaders are not sufficiently alive to the danger of their situation. . . ."[102] Conscription awakened the sleeping giant. The labour crisis deepened in 1918 as trade union spokesmen expressed the rising demands and expectations of their membership. Western leaders, increasingly disillusioned with the instrument of independent political action, turned to syndicalist and direct action tactics. And in Ontario the Independent Labor party, headed for a share of power in 1919, developed into a significant force instead of following its predecessors into the political graveyard.

[101]Robertson was a vice-president of the Railway Telegraphers while Lawrence and Nicholson were officials of the Locomotive Engineers. All were active supporters of conscription.

[102]The *Voice*, June 9, 1916.